tmux Taster

Mark McDonnell

Apress®

tmux Taster

ISBN-13 (pbk): 978-1-4842-0776-5

ISBN-13 (electronic): 978-1-4842-0775-8

Managing Director: Welmoed Spahr
Lead Editor: Louise Corrigan
Technical Reviewers: Jayant Varma, Jenna Pederson
Editorial Board: Steve Anglin, Mark Beckner, Ewan Buckingham, Gary Cornell, Louise Corrigan, Jim DeWolf, Jonathan Gennick, Robert Hutchinson, Michelle Lowman, James Markham, Matthew Moodie, Jeff Olson, Jeffrey Pepper, Douglas Pundick, Ben Renow-Clarke, Dominic Shakeshaft, Gwenan Spearing, Matt Wade, Steve Weiss
Coordinating Editor: Christine Ricketts
Copy Editor: Michael G. Laraque
Compositor: SPi Global
Indexer: SPi Global
Artist: SPi Global
Cover Designer: Anna Ishchenko

Distributed to the book trade worldwide by Springer Science+Business Media New York, 233 Spring Street, 6th Floor, New York, NY 10013. Phone 1-800-SPRINGER, fax (201) 348-4505, e-mail orders-ny@springer-sbm.com, or visit www.springeronline.com. Apress Media, LLC is a California LLC and the sole member (owner) is Springer Science + Business Media Finance Inc (SSBM Finance Inc). SSBM Finance Inc is a **Delaware** corporation.

For information on translations, please e-mail rights@apress.com, or visit www.apress.com.

Apress and friends of ED books may be purchased in bulk for academic, corporate, or promotional use. eBook versions and licenses are also available for most titles. For more information, reference our Special Bulk Sales–eBook Licensing web page at www.apress.com/bulk-sales.

Any source code or other supplementary materials referenced by the author in this text is available to readers at www.apress.com. For detailed information about how to locate your book's source code, go to www.apress.com/source-code/.

This book is dedicated to my family (Catherine, Richard, Katie, Vincent, Mum & Dad). You all know how much I love what I do, but I love you all so much more.

Contents at a Glance

Contents

About the Author

Mark McDonnell is a London-based software engineer currently working for BBC News as a senior developer. Over the past 15 years, Mark has worked his way up the ranks of the agency lifestyle. Along the way, he has built software applications in Classic ASP, ASP.NET, Flash, PHP, Node, and Ruby. He has also had the pleasure of managing and mentoring teams of highly talented developers before moving on to the BBC as a responsive front-end specialist, evolving from the client side back to the server side to work on cloud-based distributed and concurrent systems. He is a lover of the Unix philosophy and the power of the command line and always relishes the opportunity to learn new technologies. You'll normally find him chattering about functional programming with Clojure or how best to solve a technical problem, using design patterns and S.O.L.I.D principles.

About the Technical Reviewers

Jayant Varma is a technophile and was introduced to computing from the days of 8-bit computers and Z80 chips. While managing IT and Telecom at the BMW Dealerships in India and Oman and at Nissan in Qatar, he worked extensively on Windows, AS/400, and Unix. His love of traveling inspired him to work in and explore several countries, and he is currently based in Australia.

His technological journey began as a Microsoft technologies developer and has diversified to currently focus on Apple and mobile technologies. He holds a master's degree in business administration and IT from James Cook University (Australia). He also lectured at James Cook University (Australia) and coordinated the onshore and offshore teaching of Linux/Unix administration. He worked closely with the ACS (Australian Computer Society) and AUC (Apple University Consortium) on workshops and projects.

He authored the book *Learn Lua for iOS Game Development* for those about to Lua and is currently working on Swift- and iOS-related titles. As a founder, consultant, and developer at OZ Apps (www.oz-apps.com), he helps organizations and individuals integrate technology into their business and strategies. He also conducts training sessions and workshops and writes blogs to share his knowledge with the community.

Jenna Pederson became fascinated with building things at an early age. By age 13, she had run a couple of lemonade stands, a tie-dye T-shirt company, and various other businesses. She transformed her entrepreneurial drive and desire to build cool things into her career. She worked as a software engineer and technical manager before stepping out on her own in 2011. Today, Jenna runs her own company, 612 Software Foundry, helping clients translate technical needs into working software. She shares her knowledge and experience with others by presenting at tech conferences, blogging, mentoring, and volunteering.

Acknowledgments

Hello and welcome to this tmux taster book. The content you'll find within these pages was originally written as a bonus section at the end of another book I have written called *Pro Vim*. That bonus section started to expand more than I initially expected it to, and so it was decided we should extract it out into the form you find it now.

In *Pro Vim* I thanked a whole group of people for whom I've included again below; as these same people were as much a support mechanism for me writing *Pro Vim* as they were for this *tmux Taster*. So let me share with you again my thanks for their help...

I have poured a lot of time and hard work into this book, but it would be wrong of me not to acknowledge the people who have helped, either directly or indirectly, to get this book (and myself!) into the state of completion that you find it now. People such as Drew Neil, author of *Practical Vim* and the entire http://vimcasts.org/ series, whose knowledge of Vim is wide, deep, and unquestionable. If you ever find yourself in the London area, be sure to check out the Vim London events (https://twitter.com/VimLondon), which Drew kindly organizes for the community.

There is also Tim Pope, a prolific Vim plug-in creator. His work has produced a vast selection of plug-ins, which have helped make the Vim environment a much saner place. Let's take a brief moment to consider the sheer number of plug-ins he has released on which I rely daily: vim-endwise, vim-fireplace, vim-dispatch, vim-fugitive, vim-haml, vim-surround, vim-sexp-mappings-for-regular-people, vim-pathogen, vim-markdown, vim-commentary, vim-classpath, vim-repeat, vim-cucumber, timl. Phew!

Arguably, one of the most important people on this list is Simon Thulbourn (@sthulb), who is possibly *the* most sarcastic person I've ever met. (Sorry @dblooman, but you were a close second.) Before my time at the BBC, I had attempted, on a couple of occasions, to understand Vim and failed, but it was Simon who convinced me to give Vim one last try, and it was that last try that finally "broke the camel's back." Not only was I starting to make some headway with seeing myself using Vim long-term, but I also had an experienced Vim user on tap to answer questions I had when I hit a problem. I would then proceed to pester Simon on a regular basis for the next few months on every minor issue I encountered, and he would eventually (I mean graciously!) concede his valuable time to help me understand where I had gone wrong (albeit usually via the most sarcastic response he could muster). If it were not for his help, I would have likely failed for a second time, and this book would not have been.

Throughout my time at the BBC, I've had the opportunity to work with some fantastically talented developers. Dan Scotton (@danscotton) is one of those rare breeds of human being who is unbearably talented, while also being unbelievably positive and friendly. Working with Dan has been one of the highlights of my career. There is also Tom Maslen (@tmaslen) and John Cleveley (@jcleveley), neither of whom are Vim users, but don't hold that against them! I get the impression they think I'm smarter than

I actually am, but, ultimately, they gave me the chance to become part of their team, for which I'm very grateful, as it has helped me progress more in the past couple of years than I could ever have imagined.

Robert Kenny (@kenturamon) and Steven Jack (@stevenjack85) are two fellow colleagues who I've worked with at the BBC, and they, too, are keen Vim users. Both Kenny and Steve have given positive comments and encouraged this project from the beginning. They arrive here in the form of people who I greatly respect and admire and whose company I have enjoyed immensely. The amount I have learned from these two people in such a short span of time is incredible. Although the lessons I have learned from them were admittedly not directly related to the subject of Vim, they are some of the nicest and most intelligent people to spend your working hours solving complex problems with. I'm a better software engineer now, thanks to them.

Last and *most important* is the person who is my ultimate inspiration and support: my wife and soul mate, Catherine. Her tireless patience and encouragement of *everything* I do is the primary reason I have achieved one of my dreams in life. I could not have done this without her.

Introduction

The standard terminal that comes installed as part of your operating system (whether it be Mac, Linux, or Windows based) is seen by most users to be a harsh and barren wasteland, devoid of emotion and color. Respected by many a neckbeard for its power in all but a few areas where it falls short.

If you're unfamiliar with the (joke) term "neckbeard", it roughly refers to a Unix system administrator type user. You know, the type of person who has an intimate knowledge of the internals of the Linux kernel and could probably write an OS over a weekend – the sort of hardened engineer who fears no terminal environment. Even *they* have experienced times where their terminal fails to do the advanced tasks required to ease their workload; and this is where a terminal *multiplexer* steps in. The focus of this book being one particularly popular multiplexer: tmux.

At this stage I won't divulge any further details, as I cover the majority of "why use a multiplexer?" thoughts in the opening chapter of this book. But suffice to say that the information contained in this book should help you not only understand what tmux is and how to use its basic features, but it also covers customizations and abstractions; automation via a scripted interface; resolving notorious copy and paste issues; pair programming (using a tool such as Vagrant to emulate a remote server environment), as well as looking at the best ways to manage your workflow with tmux.

With all this in mind, I hope you enjoy reading *tmux Taster* and that you'll be sure to get in contact to let me know if, and how, this fantastic tool has helped you to improve your own workflow.

CHAPTER 1

■ ■ ■

Terminal Multiplexer

The terminal emulators we use on a day-to-day basis do their job admirably. Having direct access to the shell environment is a fundamental way of life for most software engineers, as it gives us a sense of power and efficiency that cannot be matched by GUI-based applications and mouse interactions.

But even a reasonably modern terminal application can fall short in many areas (such as the Terminal.app on Mac OS X). As an example, imagine your terminal window is busy with a long-running process, and you want to interact with another part of your application or project (but you want to keep an eye on the current process, so that you know when it's finished). One way you could do this is to create a new terminal tab and simply switch back and forth. This isn't a very elegant solution or efficient, but it would work.

But some terminal emulators don't let you create tabs, so if you're one of those unfortunate souls, you'll have a worse option ahead of you, which is to use your mouse to reduce the size of your terminal and then open a new instance of your terminal application and resize that new instance so you can see both terminal windows at once (that is, if you even *have* a GUI; if you don't, then . . . well, you're *almost* out of luck).

Imagine a similar (but much more typical) example: you're a software engineer and you're writing new (or modifying existing) tests for your application. Ideally, you want to be able to make changes to your tests and application code while getting immediate feedback as to whether any of those changes have broken your test suite. You want a fast feedback loop. This is where being able to split your terminal window becomes a very useful tool.

But just being able to split a window into one or more screens isn't the only problem that has to be solved. Software engineers open many different types of files during a typical workday, and sometimes, you may find yourself in a situation in which the files you have open would be easier to read and modify if they were placed in a different layout that just wasn't possible using a standard terminal emulator.

In Figure 1-1, we can see we're not just splitting a terminal window into equal-sized chunks. We have window C, which spans the full width of the screen, while windows D, E, and F are a third of the overall screen, and windows A, B, G, and H split 50% of the available screen dimensions.

```
-------------------------------------------------
|       A       |         B         |
-------------------------------------------------
|               C                   |
-------------------------------------------------
|       D   |   E   |   F           |
-------------------------------------------------
|       G       |       H           |
-------------------------------------------------
```

Figure 1-1. *Example of a complex layout of terminal windows*

We also want to be able to manipulate these windows very easily, through shorthand key bindings, and change their dimensions (and even change the layout of the windows, so that they are rearranged into a different format, to fit with the work we do later on in the day).

Humans are also creatures of habit, meaning that there will be a particular layout of windows that we find works best for us 90% of the time, and, so, being able to automate the creation of a particular layout is another feature that would be useful.

Finally, a tool that has the capability to allow me to share my screen seamlessly, so that I can pair program with another individual and have him/her take over the typing on my machine, is incredibly useful when you're a remote worker.

Having complete control over our terminal environment—how it looks and behaves—is a very powerful idea, and one that is possible through the use of an application called tmux. In the next section, I'll explain a little about what tmux is and means, as well as how to install and configure it.

▓ **Note**   Some readers may have heard of a recent terminal emulator called iTerm2 (`http://iterm2.com` [for Mac OS X only]), which allows you to make split windows (among other features) but suffers from much less ubiquity than my tool of choice: tmux. For example, if I'm on a remote Linux server, I can quickly download and install tmux and be up and running. I can't do that with a program that is limited to a single operating system. As with Vim, a popular terminal based text editor, ubiquity is the key.

---

tmux

tmux is short for [*t*]*erminal* [*mu*]*ltiple*[*x*]*er*. A multiplexer is simply a fancy way of describing an application that lets you easily manage multiple terminal windows within one screen.

tmux runs a server/client architecture, meaning that when you start the application, it will fire up a single server, and every tmux instance you create on your machine will ultimately connect to that single tmux server. The benefit of this design is that while your machine is running, you can *detach* a tmux "session" (i.e., close tmux but keep the details of that session open, as it'll be stored on the tmux server running in a background process), so you can then *reattach* to the session at another time.

▒ **Note**   Visit http://tmux.sourceforge.net/ for frequently asked questions and helpful information (such as documentation, IRC, and mailing list details), as well as to download binaries of the software.

---

tmux provides a lot of powerful features (most of which were described indirectly via the introduction of this chapter), which I've summarized into a few categories following:

- Ability to connect to existing local and remote sessions
- Advanced window and pane management
- Ability to move windows between different sessions
- Scripted automation

The usefulness of tmux truly reveals itself once you start utilizing it on a day-to-day basis and incorporating it firmly into your workflow. By the time we're finished, you should have a much better understanding of the power and flexibility tmux provides and will wonder how you ever managed without it.

Terminology

Let's take a brief detour to consider the terminology we'll be using to describe tmux's functionality. This will help to understand different tmux concepts as we move through the following chapters.

Prefix Command

The purpose of a multiplexer is to help you load multiple programs within a single window. Because you are effectively loading a program *within* a program (e.g., loading Vim inside a tmux window), tmux must avoid command conflicts with the subprograms being loaded. To do this, it introduces the concept of a prefix command, which helps to differentiate tmux commands from other programs you use.

▒ **Note**   The default prefix for tmux commands is <C-b>. You'll notice that we shorten references to keyboard shortcuts. The principle is as follows: pressing the keys <Ctrl> and b at the same time can be represented as <C-b>. Similarly, pressing the keys <Esc> and 1 can be expressed as <Esc-1>. If we need to press any further keys, for example, let's say we need to press <Ctrl> and b at the same time followed by d, then we express that as <C-b>d

---

Let's take a look at a quick example, to clarify what the prefix command does and why. I appreciate that we have yet to even open tmux, but the concept of a prefix key is fundamental to using tmux in the first place, and so I'm hoping you'll indulge me for just a moment longer, while I attempt to explain it.

Imagine we have tmux running, and for those who have never seen tmux before, you'll likely not notice much difference in your terminal's appearance (other than a bar at the foot of your screen, but I'll come back to this and describe what the bar is and what it means later), because visually, tmux should act as a container *around* your terminal.

Now, let's say we want to open a text file within the popular Vim text editor (e.g., `vim ~/foo.txt`) and modify the content by deleting a specific selection. Chances are you would open the file in Vim, find the content you want to delete, select it, and execute the d command (which is Vim's delete command). The problem with this process is that tmux assigns its own functionality to the d key (a command for detaching from a session; again, if this doesn't make sense, don't worry too much for now, as I'll cover sessions in due time). This is a perfect example of why tmux commands have a prefix: to avoid conflicts with other programs loaded within a tmux screen.

Due to tmux commands having a prefix, we can safely use Vim (or any other program) and not have to worry that executing a command within our subprograms will cause a side effect in tmux. In the previous scenario, we would detach from our tmux session using the command `<C-b>d` (where `<C-b>` is the prefix, followed by the d to indicate we wish to *detach* from the session).

Throughout the rest of the book, I'll refer to the prefix key `<C-b>` as just `<P>` (for [P]*refix*). This means the structure of all tmux commands in this book will take the form `<P>{key-binding|:command-prompt}`. In the preceding example, in which we detached from the tmux session using the key binding `<C-b>d`, we would represent this using `<P>d` (see the following note regarding the "command prompt").

▓ **Note**   tmux provides a "command prompt" (similar in ways to Vim's COMMAND-LINE/Ex modes), which you can access by using `<P>:`, followed by a command. For example, `<P>:{command}`.

The reason for shortening the prefix command in the following chapters is, first, to make the commands shorter and easier to read, but more important, I'll be showing you how you can change the prefix key to be any key combination you like. So if you end up using this book as a reference, and you happen to have changed the prefix to be something else (let's say `<C-a>`), it would be easier to mentally replace `<C-b>` with your own prefix.

Help?

Unfortunately, if you need help with tmux commands, you don't have as rich a support feature as found in other programs, such as the Vim text editor (whose built-in `:help` documentation are very detailed and useful), but there are still a few options available to you, which are useful to know about.

Command and Key Binding References

tmux provides a quick reference list of all available key bindings, which you can access either via a key binding or the command-line prompt (or even from outside tmux itself).

To access the key binding reference via a key binding, you would use <P>?. To access this reference via the command prompt, you would use <P>:list-keys. Finally, you can also access this list from *outside* of tmux, using tmux list-keys (allowing you to utilize this information in some form of scripted automation, which I'll cover in more detail in Chapter 6).

The list-keys command will only display a list of available tmux key bindings. This does not include all commands that are executable within the tmux command prompt. For that list, you would use <P>:list-commands (or tmux list-commands, if you're outside of tmux); there is no key binding variation.

If you would like to see some extra information regarding each of the tmux sessions you have open, the following command will display this information for you: <P>:info (or tmux info, if you're outside of tmux).

Manual

Although the Internet has lots of useful information about how to do certain things in tmux, ultimately, the best resource of documentation is the official manual, which is linked to from the tmux web site and is directly accessible at www.openbsd.org/cgi-bin/man.cgi/OpenBSD-current/man1/tmux.1.

Alternatively, and more usefully, you can access this documentation via your terminal, using the command man tmux (which also makes it much easier to filter and search through).

Message Feedback

One annoyance with tmux is when you execute a command incorrectly. What you'll notice happen is that tmux *tries* to be helpful by displaying a message telling you the correct format of the command it thinks you were trying to execute. But, unfortunately, that message only displays for a fraction of a second and then disappears, not leaving you enough time to see what the requirements of the command actually are.

Luckily, tmux provides a key binding that shows us the complete list of messages tmux has passed to us during our current session (the list of messages is displayed in ascending order, so the oldest messages are at the top, and the most recent at the bottom): <P>~. (You can also access this feature via the command prompt <P>:show-messages.)

Installation and Configuration

I mentioned earlier that one of the benefits of using tmux over other solutions is its ubiquity across different platforms. Installing tmux is remarkably simple for such a powerful and distributed piece of software, as we can see in the following options.

Mac

To install tmux on Mac OS X, the simplest option is to use the popular Homebrew package manager (`http://brew.sh/`):

```
brew install tmux
```

Linux

If you're working from a Linux machine, then use your package manager of choice (e.g. Apt, Yum etc). For example, if you're using Apt then you would run the following command:

```
sudo apt-get install tmux
```

▦ **Note**   At the time of writing, the majority of package managers only have version 1.8 available. If you wish to install a more recent version of tmux then you'll need to modify your package manager to point to another registry where tmux can be acquired. As an example, for Apt you would first execute `add-apt-repository ppa:pi-rho/dev` followed by `apt-get update` and finally execute the install command `apt-get install tmux`

Windows

If you're on a Windows machine, you can install tmux as a Cygwin package.

▦ **Note**   If Cygwin is already installed, you'll have to rerun `setup.exe` and make sure to select the tmux package.

Configuring tmux

tmux can be configured to work however you require it to. You can change the way it looks, the key bindings it uses, and many different additional optional settings. This configuration is primarily handled by a .tmux.conf file, usually placed within your $HOME directory (e.g., ~/ but can be moved using a symlink).

By the time we're finished in this chapter, and you have tmux open for the first time, you should see something similar to Figure 1-2.

Figure 1-2. *Expected tmux view, if using the configuration file described in this chapter*

In the following section I'll show you the contents of my own .tmux.conf file (and I'll assume you're using it too). After I show you the file contents, I'll break down each part of it, so that you can decide if you would like to use/keep the specific settings or not.

■ **Note**   It may actually be better to skip this section until you've reached the end of the book. That way, you'll have more experience with the features of tmux to make a judgment about what settings you want to keep within your own configuration. There is no harm, however, in reading through this now, if you're interested!

```
unbind C-b
set -g prefix C-Space

bind-key L last-window

bind-key -r h select-pane -L
bind-key -r j select-pane -D
bind-key -r k select-pane -U
bind-key -r l select-pane -R

bind-key Up    select-pane -U
bind-key Down  select-pane -D
bind-key Left  select-pane -L
bind-key Right select-pane -R

bind-key v split-window -h
bind-key s split-window -v

bind-key r source-file ~/.tmux.conf

bind-key -n C-k clear-history

bind-key < resize-pane -L 5
bind-key > resize-pane -R 5
bind-key + resize-pane -U 5
bind-key - resize-pane -D 5
bind-key = select-layout even-vertical
bind-key | select-layout even-horizontal

set -g default-terminal "screen-256color"

set-window-option -g utf8 on
set -g status on
set -g status-utf8 on

set-option -g status-keys vi

setw -g mode-keys vi

set -sg escape-time 0

set-option -g allow-rename off

set-option -g default-shell /bin/zsh

set -g base-index 1
```

```
set -g history-limit 30000

set-option -g renumber-windows on

set -g status-right '#[fg=colour234,bg=white,nobold,nounderscore,
noitalics]◀#[fg=colour250,bg=colour234] %a #[fg=colour247,bg=colour234]◁
#[fg=colour247,bg=colour234] %b %d ◁ %R #[fg=colour252,bg=colour234,nobold,
nounderscore,noitalics]#[fg=red,bg=colour234]◀#[fg=white,bg=red] #H'
set -g status-bg white
set -g status-justify 'left'
set -g pane-border-fg white
set -g pane-active-border-fg red
set -g message-bg red
set -g message-fg white
setw -g window-status-separator '  '
setw -g window-status-current-format '#[fg=colour231,bg=colour31,bold]
#I ▷ #W #[fg=colour31,bg=white,nobold,nounderscore,noitalics]▶'
```

■ **Note**   In the preceding code snippet you'll notice some some symbols that we use to help improve the design of our tmux status bar, such as ◀ and ▷. If you were to look at the .tmux.conf file on GitHub (https://github.com/Integralist/ProVim/blob/master/.tmux.conf) you'll likely see a different symbol. This is because the display of the icon will depend on whether you have UTF-8 enabled and the relevant font installed. The font you need is Ubuntu Mono derivative Powerline.ttf and you can download this font from the above GitHub repository as well. The repository also includes a Mac OS based terminal theme file I use. Once you install that theme you'll need to change the font setting to the font mentioned above.

Change the Default Prefix

In the following code snippet, we're changing the default prefix command to <C-Space>. This is an important setting that I personally find makes a positive difference in my use of tmux.

I typically find that on a laptop (and certain external keyboards), the default prefix of <C-b> is too awkward to use on a day-to-day basis. I've tried many variations, such as <C-a>, and even just `, as my prefix key, but none of them was as comfortable as <C-Space>. (This also means, as I'm a heavy Vim user, that my little finger is conveniently placed on the <Ctrl> key ready for a <C-w> command to be fired off.)

```
unbind C-b
set -g prefix C-Space
```

As you can see, we're first unbinding the default prefix <C-b>, then we're resetting the prefix globally (-g) to <C-Space>.

Quick Access to Last Window

If you find yourself jumping around different tmux windows a lot, you'll realize the benefit of a simple binding, such as the following code snippet demonstrates, which lets you quickly jump back to the last window you were just in (saving you from having to remember the identifier number of the window).

I'll cover what "windows" and "panes" mean in the context of tmux (and how they work), in the following chapters, so don't worry too much about them now. If it helps, just think of windows as equivalent to tabs you use in your web browser, and panes as dividing your visible screen up into individual pieces (each piece is its own terminal).

```
bind-key L last-window
```

Vim Style Movements

The following code snippet allows me to use similar bindings to those found in the Vim text editor (i.e. Vim's home row keys) when moving to and from different panes. I actually don't use these bindings that much, as I prefer to use the arrow keys (see the following section).

```
bind-key -r h select-pane -L
bind-key -r j select-pane -D
bind-key -r k select-pane -U
bind-key -r l select-pane -R
```

Again, we're using tmux's bind-key function to create the custom binding of <P>{h|j|k|l}, and those bindings end up running tmux's select-pane function, with its corresponding flag to indicate the direction of the pane to be selected.

The -r flag tells tmux that the command is allowed to be recursive. This simply means that when the prefix command is hit, and the user then presses one of the keys h, j, k, or l, he/she can press one of those keys *again*, to cause the action to be triggered one more time.

▓ **Note** The amount of times you can press on a custom key binding that has been set to "recursive" depends on the repeat-time configuration (default value is 500ms). See the tmux manual for more information.

In other words, if I had three tmux panes (with my focus being on the pane farthest left of the screen), and I wanted to move to the one farthest right, then I could execute <P>ll (thus moving two panes to the right), and this would be more efficient than executing <P>l<P>l.

Arrow Movements

The following bindings I use a lot! I find these much more useful and efficient than executing the relevant `select-pane` commands within tmux's command prompt (that would become hideously tedious).

```
bind-key Up    select-pane -U
bind-key Down  select-pane -D
bind-key Left  select-pane -L
bind-key Right select-pane -R
```

Simpler Pane Creation

I don't use the following key bindings any more. I used to use them a lot, but I found myself getting caught out when working from a tmux configuration that wasn't my own (e.g., remote server work or pair programming with a colleague), and so I decided it was just easier to memorize the default <P>" and <P>% command (we'll see these bindings again in later chapters).

```
bind-key v split-window -h
bind-key s split-window -v
```

Source .tmux.conf

I don't use the following binding very often, but it is handy to have included in your configuration, as it makes it very quick and easy to reload your `.tmux.conf` file, if you've made a change to it.

```
bind-key r source-file ~/.tmux.conf
```

Clear Pane History

I would say that I've probably used this feature once in my entire tmux career! I've included it here simply for the sake of completeness (as you may find the need for it that I never did). The binding does exactly what you might expect: the current pane has its command history removed.

```
bind-key -n C-k clear-history
```

Easier Pane Management

Being able to easily resize panes (you'll notice we use the `resize-pane` function and pass through a default of five columns/rows) and balance out my layouts (I'll explain this in a moment) are essential tools for my day-to-day workflow.

```
bind-key < resize-pane -L 5
bind-key > resize-pane -R 5
bind-key + resize-pane -U 5
bind-key - resize-pane -D 5
bind-key = select-layout even-vertical
bind-key | select-layout even-horizontal
```

The last two bindings use tmux's even-vertical and even-horizontal layout feature, to help balance the many panes you might have open, so that they have equal distribution (i.e., each pane is made the same size).

For example, take a look at Figure 1-3, which demonstrates what a typical tmux session might look like (many different sized panes open), then take a look at Figure 1-4, to see what the even-vertical command does to that layout. Finally, take a look at Figure 1-5, to see what the even-horizontal command does to the layout.

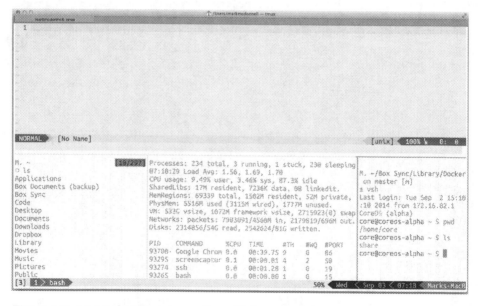

Figure 1-3. *A typical tmux session, with multiple panes open*

As you can see from Figure 1-3, we have multiple panes open (again, I'll cover how to create panes soon enough in another chapter), which utilize a different process in each pane.

The top pane has Vim open, and the bottom left pane is displaying the result of running the ls command, while the bottom middle pane is displaying the result of running the top command (and so it isn't static content but updates regularly, as you would expect). The last pane is an SSH session into a CoreOS Linux box I have built on my laptop (made available by the use of Vagrant, which is a tool for allowing quick and easy creation of reproducible development environments—www.vagrantup.com).

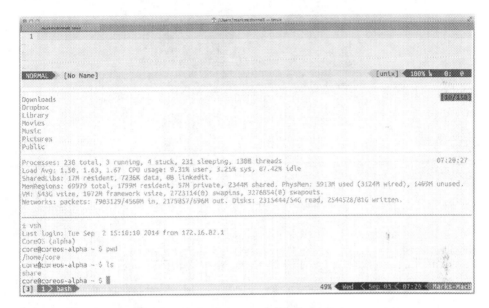

Figure 1-4. *The same tmux session with* even-vertical *applied*

In Figure 1-4, we can see the result of the key binding <P>=, which actually triggers tmux's select-layout function, and we pass it the value of even-vertical. You should also notice that the result is panes that are vertically stacked evenly on top of each other (as even-vertical suggests).

■ **Note** I chose the = character for this custom key binding, as it adequately represents the result of the even-vertical option.

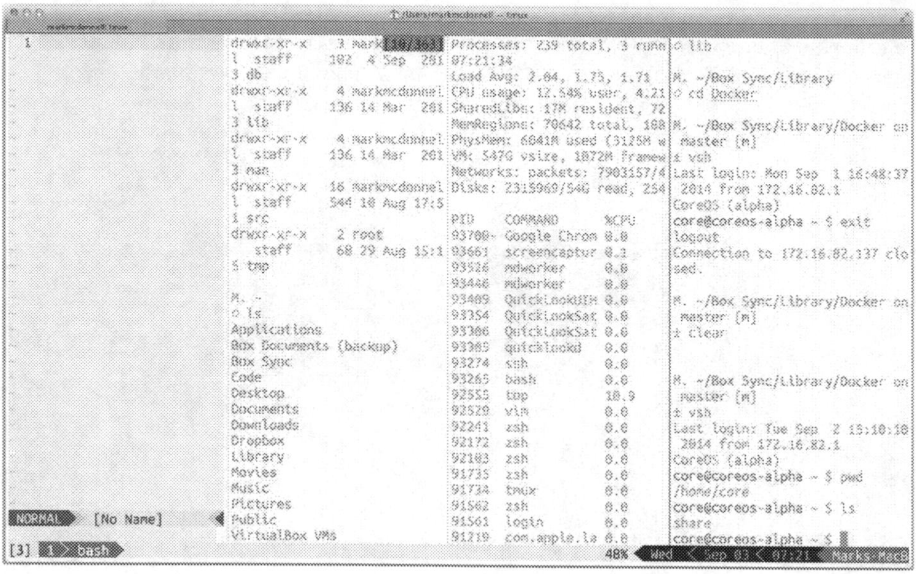

Figure 1-5. *The same tmux session with even-horizontal applied*

In Figure 1-5, we can see the result of the key binding <P>|, which actually triggers tmux's select-layout function, and we pass it the value of even-horizontal. You should also notice that the result is panes that are horizontally stacked evenly next to each other (as even-horizontal suggests).

■ **Note**   I chose the | character for this custom key binding, as it adequately represents the result of the even-horizontal option.

Color Correction

To ensure that tmux uses the correct color profile, we can inform tmux what the color support is for our terminal emulator application, by changing the value of the default-terminal option to be a derivative of "screen," in this case, that our terminal supports 256 colors.

Although I have this setting in place, it's strictly not needed, as the default value for the TERM environment variable will ensure that tmux loads the right color profile (but only certain versions of Mac OS X have 256-color support, so you may have to tweak this value to suit your OS requirements).

```
set -g default-terminal "screen-256color"
```

Enable utf8

We use a specific font (Ubuntu Mono derivative Powerline.ttf, downloadable from https://github.com/Integralist/ProVim/) to control the look of our tmux status bar (see the "Change the Status Bar Appearing" section, following), and because of this, if we don't enable utf8 support in tmux, those characters won't display properly in the tmux status bar.

```
set-window-option -g utf8 on
set -g status on
set -g status-utf8 on
```

Command Prompt Movements

The status-key option lets us modify how we move our cursor around while typing within the tmux command prompt (e.g., the command prompt is accessed using <P>:), meaning, if we set the value to vi, we can utilize some basic Vi motions.

If we enter the command prompt and type some text (or, more appropriately, some tmux commands), we can press <Esc> and then use some basic Vi style motions, such as w, e, and b, to move around, and i, to start typing again.

```
set-option -g status-keys vi
```

Cancel Immediately

I like to set the escape-time setting to zero, so that anytime I press <Esc>, that action is triggered immediately. If I don't have this setting, tmux will wait a fraction of a second to make sure that <Esc> isn't being executed as part of a sequence of commands.

```
set -sg escape-time 0
```

Prevent Program Window Renaming Trigger

tmux tries to be helpful by renaming the window tab to represent the process that is currently running. I don't like that behavior, as I prefer to manually rename my window tabs (I'll cover how to do this in an upcoming chapter).

As an example, if I were in a normal directory, the window tab would be renamed to Zsh, to represent that I'm in a shell environment. If I were to start up a Pry session (Pry is a Ruby CLI REPL tool), because I use JRuby (a Java implementation of the Ruby programming language), then the underlying process would be Java, and so my window tab would be renamed java.

After disabling this setting, if I manually rename my window tab to Foo, then no matter what I do or open in that window, the window tab will continue using the same name that I gave to it.

```
set-option -g allow-rename off
```

Change the Default Shell

This is a setting I don't necessarily need to have, but I like to be explicit and keep it in. The default value is determined by the SHELL environment variable, which for me is set to /bin/zsh and means that for all new windows you open in tmux, it will use that shell as its default.

```
set-option -g default-shell /bin/zsh
```

Human Numbering

All tmux windows (by default) are indexed from zero, which I find highly irritating, as there is no reason for it to be that way. This setting fixes this problem, by forcing tmux to index windows by starting from the number one.

```
set -g base-index 1
```

Increase Scroll-back

When scrolling tmux's screen buffer (don't worry if you don't understand what that means right now, as I'll cover it in the next chapter), we can't keep scrolling forever. There is a limit of 2000 buffer lines that tmux will store in its history. Certain processes can easily produce output that exceeds this limit, meaning we will find ourselves scrolling through a large stack trace error, and we'll stop halfway through the output, as we can't scroll back any further in the buffer's history. To resolve this issue, we can increase this limit, using the history-limit option.

```
set -g history-limit 30000
```

Automatic Window Renumbering

You'll see in an upcoming chapter how to create new windows, and in doing so, you'll notice that tmux automatically numbers each window (starting from the base-index). If we had three windows open, then the windows would be numbered 1, 2, and 3 (with the assumption that the base-index option was set to 1).

If we removed the second window, the default result would be two remaining windows, numbered 1 and 3. But with the renumber-windows option turned on, this would mean tmux could automatically renumber the windows to 1 and 2.

```
set-option -g renumber-windows on
```

Change the Status Bar Appearing

It seems the first thing most tmux users want to do is to configure the appearance of their tmux status bar. It is the source of a lot of information, and so I can appreciate that users are passionate about getting it to look perfect for their needs.

In Figure 1-6, we can see what the tmux status bar will look like when using the preceding .tmux.conf configuration. Let's take a moment to review the different parts of the status bar that we've styled.

- [test]: This is the name of the tmux session.

- 1 > zsh: This indicates there is one window running a Zsh shell.

- 83%: This is my battery percentage.

- Wed < Sep 03 < 17:54: This is the current date and time.

- Marks-MacB: This is the name of my computer.

Figure 1-6. *The tmux status bar redesigned by our* .tmux.conf *configuration*

Following is the relevant code inside the .tmux.conf file that creates this status bar:

```
set -g status-right '#[fg=colour234,bg=white,nobold,nounderscore,
noitalics]◀#[fg=colour250,bg=colour234] %a #[fg=colour247,bg=colour234]
◁#[fg=colour247,bg=colour234] %b %d ◁ %R #[fg=colour252,bg=colour234,nobold,
nounderscore,noitalics]#[fg=red,bg=colour234]◀#[fg=white,bg=red] #H'
set -g status-bg white
set -g status-justify 'left'
set -g pane-border-fg white
set -g pane-active-border-fg red
set -g message-bg red
set -g message-fg white
setw -g window-status-separator ' '
setw -g window-status-current-format '#[fg=colour231,bg=colour31,bold]
#I ▷ #W #[fg=colour31,bg=white,nobold,nounderscore,noitalics]▶'
```

■ **Note** The battery percentage you see in Figure 1-6 is a custom setting that I've not included within the preceding .tmux.conf file, because it requires an external script that has been untested on Linux/Windows. For more details, visit https://github.com/richo/battery/.

Summary

So, this introduction to tmux has been quite fast-paced. I hope you're now even more excited to reach the upcoming chapters and discover more about how to use tmux. With your custom configuration in place, you can move on to learning some of the more practical uses of tmux. Let's quickly recap some of the things we've seen so far.

- We began by considering some of the failures of standard terminal emulators and how tmux can help solve those issues.

- I explained the meaning behind the name *tmux* and what the architecture pattern is (i.e., a server/client model), including the ability to attach, detach, and reattach to preexisting sessions.

- Next, I covered the tmux terminology (such as the prefix command), so you have a clear language to help you understand the upcoming chapters.

- I also briefly covered the different ways you can get help with tmux.

- Last, we looked at installing and configuring tmux, followed by a breakdown of the example tmux configuration file.

CHAPTER 2

■ ■ ■

Fundamentals

In the previous chapter, we became acquainted with the concept of tmux and what this program could offer us in the way of resolving some standard terminal emulator annoyances. In this chapter, we're going to start using tmux and investigate some of its different constructs and terminology, such as the following:

- Sessions
- Buffers
- Panes
- Windows

By the end of this chapter, you'll know enough about tmux to be a confident user and start integrating it into your workflow. There will still be much more to learn (and after this chapter, we'll start to investigate tmux's other features), but for now, consider what you learn here to be an essential and solid foundation upon which we'll be building.

Sessions

tmux is designed around the idea of a "client-server" model (this introduces three new terminologies: client, server, and session), and this means that when we start tmux (from our terminal application), we're effectively using the tmux *client*. The client will attempt to create a new *session* on the tmux *server*, and if a server doesn't exist, one will be started up in a background process to which our client can connect.

Within a session, we can do anything we could do normally within the terminal environment. The only difference is that, now, all our activity is recorded within a tmux session.

Let's consider a quick example that demonstrates why sessions are so useful. We start work in the morning by opening a new tmux session. In this session, we'll be working on our company's latest project, "X." But after lunch, we realize that although we're not quite finished with what we needed to get done, we have to jump onto an older project, "A," so we can fix some critical bug. In this scenario, we currently have quite a few tmux "windows" and "panes" open (I'll explain these features later on in this chapter, but for now, consider them similar to the tabs in your web browser and dividing your screen up into multiple sections). It would be nice if we could keep our entire working environment in place, so that we can move on to this other project, and then when done with "A," we can come back and reinstate the entire "X" environment exactly as we left it.

This type of scenario occurs more often than you probably realize, and although there are ways to work around it without the use of tmux, they're not as elegant (as you'll see). The reason we have this power to detach and attach sessions at our leisure is because of tmux's client-server model, which means that while our computer is running, the tmux server will stay alive (thus keeping open all the different sessions we've created).

Creating a Session

To create a new tmux session, we run the tmux command from our terminal application. Doing this will create and connect to a new session that is automatically named by tmux (unless you provide a name; see Figure 2-1).

Figure 2-1. *Example of a new tmux session (automatically numbered)*

▓ **Note**   tmux sessions are named numerically by default. So if you run tmux, it will create a session whose identifier is 0. If you were to run the tmux command again in another terminal, the next session would be identified as session 1 (and so forth).

To help distinguish between different sessions you have running, you can give them a descriptive name. To do this, you can run the following command:

```
tmux new -s my_session
```

In the preceding example, we use the -s flag to indicate that we want to give the session we're about to create the name "my_session." When you start a new session, you are automatically connected to it, but you can start new sessions and not connect, by adding the -d flag, which indicates a "detached" state, as follows:

```
tmux new -s my_session -d
```

Listing Sessions

When you have multiple sessions open, it can be hard to remember them all, so tmux provides a complete list of every session you have created. To view the session list (Figure 2-2), you can run one of the following commands:

- tmux ls (from outside tmux)

- <P>:list-sessions (from inside a current tmux session)

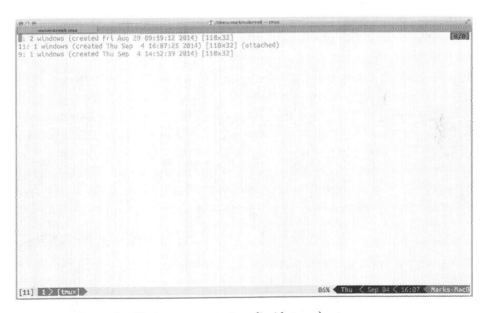

Figure 2-2. Example of listing current sessions (inside tmux)

When using the latter command, the list will be displayed within the current tmux pane. To close the list, simply press <CR>.

Selecting a Session

If you have multiple sessions open and you want to jump around the different sessions currently available, tmux makes this very easy, by providing not only commands that can be executed via the command prompt but also custom key bindings. (Admittedly, I personally don't have much need for this type of feature, but, hey, it's interesting nonetheless, I think).

The following command will list all available sessions and allow you to use the arrow keys to navigate the list and select the session you wish to move to, by pressing <CR> when your cursor is placed on the relevant session you want to open (see Figure 2-3 for the output):

```
:choose-session
```

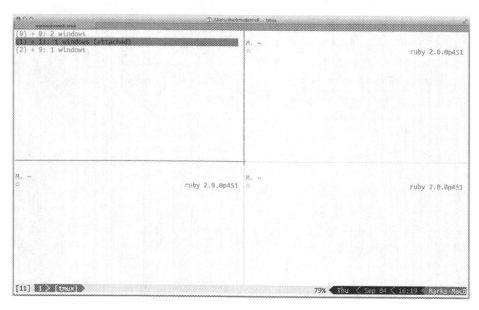

Figure 2-3. *Example of running* `:choose-session` *inside a single pane*

▓ **Note** The current session is automatically highlighted.

The following key bindings will also allow you to move through all sessions sequentially:

- <P>(: Move to next session
- <P>): Move to previous session

Renaming Sessions

Most of the time, when I create a new session, I'm being lazy (and/or forgetful), and I won't specify a name for my session. When I come back to look at what sessions I have open (so I know what session I want to go back to), it can be tricky to determine what session holds what project, if they're all just numerically identified.

In such instances, it can be helpful to rename your sessions, so that they become more descriptive of what they hold. This can be done while inside of tmux, using the <P>$ command. Doing so will drop you into tmux's command prompt, allowing you to enter a new name.

■ **Note**   You can access this feature from the command prompt by using <P> and then typing :rename-session -t {current_id} {new_id}. You can also access this feature (as with other command prompt-based commands) from outside tmux, using tmux rename-session -t {current_id} {new_id}.

Closing vs. Detaching

Because tmux uses a client-server model, we can close our client but still keep the session open and running. There are a couple of commands that are easily mixed up (a command to detach from the session and another for actually closing the session). They may be similar, but they do have subtle but very important differences that you need to be aware of.

- If you have multiple panes open, executing exit or <C-d> within the terminal shell (for that pane) will cause the pane to be closed. (If you have multiple panes open, then the remaining panes will stay open until you run the same command within those panes).

- If you only have one pane open within a window, executing exit or <C-d> within the terminal shell (for that pane) will cause the pane/window to be closed. If you have only one window, the entire session will be closed. (If you have multiple windows open, only that window will be closed).

- Executing <P>d from any pane or window will cause the tmux client to detach from the current session.

Application Bootstrap

tmux also allows us to create a new session and have it start up automatically inside a program of our choosing. The following command demonstrates how we can start a new session that automatically opens the Vim text editor program:

```
tmux new -s my_session vim
```

▓ **Note** This only works with a single application. This means you can't specify multiple programs to be opened, without using more advanced automation commands (which we'll see in Chapter 6) as tmux doesn't know how to handle multiple programs. For example, if there were two programs specified – tmux new vim top – then tmux won't know how to load both of them (vim and top).

Buffers

When you establish a tmux session, you're presented with a *viewport* to the standard terminal screen. Effectively, it doesn't look like much has changed (if it weren't for the tmux status bar now appearing at the bottom of the screen). This viewport is referred to as a *buffer* (specifically an "output buffer"). What this means is that any information presented to you is actually farmed off to stdout, which, in this case, is your terminal screen.

Scrolling the Buffer

Because this is just a viewport, if there was too much information to display and it didn't fit in your current screen, it would appear "off screen," and you would have to scroll back up the screen to see the content you missed. For us to scroll the buffer so that we can see the additional content that didn't fit our screen, we have to execute a command that puts us into tmux's "copy mode," as follows:

<P>[

▓ **Note** Just to reiterate, as all key binding commands can also be accessed via the command prompt, so copy mode can be accessed by executing <P>:, followed by typing copy-mode.

You'll know when you're in copy mode by the fact of tmux displaying a counter in the top right of the screen (Figure 2-4). This counter will look something like [0/28441] (it'll change depending on context).

Figure 2-4. *tmux in copy mode, indicated by top-right scroll position*

To explain what the counter represents, let's consider the preceding example. In the example, I ran the command `tree`, to display the tree structure of all files and folders within my $HOME directory. This means there is lots of content that is impossible to fit onto a single screen, and so it appears outside the screen viewport. When I entered into copy mode, it displays the counter [0/28441], which tells us that there are currently 28441 buffer lines that have scrolled off the screen. The first number (0 in this case) is the current offscreen line.

That might not make much sense, so let's demonstrate what I mean by that explanation. At the moment, while in copy mode, I'm at the bottom of the visible buffer. There are 28441 lines of the buffer currently offscreen. If I use the up arrow key to move up the buffer, the first number will stay set to 0, until I reach the top of the viewport. Once my cursor moves one line *beyond* the viewport, you'll see that the number zero changes to 1, and then for every line after that I go upward, it increases, until I reach the top of the buffer itself, where the number will stop at 28441 (as I've reached the top of the offscreen buffer content).

Navigating Copy Mode

You can navigate the copy mode by using both arrow keys, as well as the standard Vim key bindings `hjkl`. If you want to jump directly to a specific offscreen line, use the following command: `:{line_number}`. So if you wanted to jump to the 50th line outside the viewport, you would execute `:50`.

▨ **Note**   This command doesn't require the prefix, so it's not `<P>:50` but, literally, consists of pressing `:`, followed by the line number (while in copy mode).

You can also use familiar Vim bindings such as gg and G to move to the top and bottom, respectively, of the buffer content. The tmux copy mode also provides both a forward and backward search facility similar to Vim, as follows:

- `/{search_phrase}` = search *forward* through the buffer

- `?{search_phrase}` = search *backward* through the buffer

To exit copy mode you can press either one of the following keys:

- `<CR>`

- `q`

Panes

In tmux, the "panes" feature effectively splits the current viewport into subsections. Each split of the screen is referred to as its own *pane* and contains a new shell instance for us to work from.

When tmux connects to a session, you will note that you begin with a single window (and, thus, a single pane inside that window). The window is also referred to as the *viewport*.

To split the window into separate panes, you'll need to decide whether you want to split it into either a horizontal or vertical pane. To split the viewport into two panes that sit horizontally to each other, you would execute one of the following commands:

- `<P>:split-window -h`

- `<P>%`

To split the viewport into two panes that sit vertically to each other, you would execute one of the following commands:

- `<P>:split-window -v`

- `<P>"`

▨ **Note**   Remember to check the `.tmux.conf` file from the previous chapter (also available online `https://github.com/Integralist/ProVim/blob/master/.tmux.conf`), as you'll find some custom key bindings that replace `<P>%` and `<P>"` with `<P>v` and `<P>s`, which feels more at home for Vim users (although I personally prefer to use the default bindings).

Closing

As I mentioned earlier, to close a pane, you just have to run the command <C-d> or type exit; but these only work when any programs in the pane are closed, and we're back in the terminal shell. What happens, though, if we have to force-close a pane? I have had this problem quite a few times when running certain applications that have hit a fatal error and can't use either <C-c> or <C-d> to stop them.

In those instances, running the <P>x command will act as a "force quit." It'll display a message (within the command prompt) asking if we would like to "kill-pane {pane_number}? (y/n)," to which the response would be y, for *yes*.

Navigating

tmux makes splitting the current window viewport into multiple panes very easy and inexpensive, but it does offer a few different ways to navigate your pane layout. There is a simple sequential command that effectively rotates you through each pane in a sequence (e.g., moving in one direction), until you reach the pane you want to work inside. Using the <P>o command does this.

There is also a command prompt variation that allows you to move in any direction. The following list demonstrates moving left, right, up, and down:

- <P>:select-pane -L
- <P>:select-pane -R
- <P>:select-pane -U
- <P>:select-pane -D

The command prompt version of a command can be quite tedious to execute, so it's best to create a set of custom key bindings to help make this task a little quicker and easier. If you have the .tmux.conf configuration file from the previous chapter, then you'll find that includes the following custom bindings:

```
# Vim style
bind-key -r h select-pane -L
bind-key -r j select-pane -D
bind-key -r k select-pane -U
bind-key -r l select-pane -R

# Arrow keys
bind-key Up    select-pane -U
bind-key Down  select-pane -D
bind-key Left  select-pane -L
bind-key Right select-pane -R
```

We can also jump straight to any pane we want to focus on by running the <P>q command. When executed, this command will display a numeric value on top of each pane. While the numbers are visible, you will be able to specify the pane you want to move your cursor inside of, by simply typing the relevant number.

▓ **Note** The numeric identifiers for each pane only appear for a brief moment, and jumping to a pane only works while they are visible. So, act quickly and press the number of the pane you want to jump to while the identifiers are on screen.

The <P>q command is again a key binding built into tmux that simply executes the command prompt variation :display-panes (see Figure 2-5). So, if you're looking to do some kind of scripted automation of tmux (which I'll cover in a later chapter), being aware of the command prompt versions can be useful.

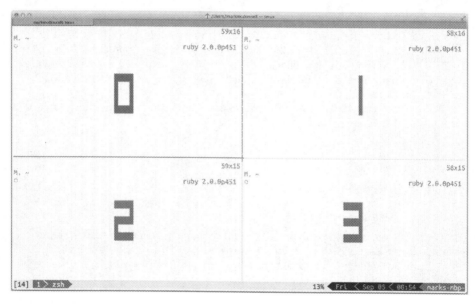

Figure 2-5. *Result of tmux* :display-panes *command (before confirming selection)*

Resizing

To resize a pane in tmux, you'll need the :resize-pane command. The following is an example of its syntax structure:

<P>:resize-pane -t {pane_id} -D {amount}

In the preceding example, we're telling tmux to target (-t) the pane we want to resize (replace {pane_id} with a numeric id value), and then we tell it what direction (-d) to resize and what amount to resize by (replace {amount} with a numeric value).

For all details of this command, see the documentation, but for the majority of users, the following flags/options are what they need to know:

- -U: Resize window upward.

- -D: Resize window downward.

- -L: Resize window to the left.

- -R: Resize window to the right.

There is also a slightly simpler form, in which you can leave off the target, and tmux will assume you want to resize the current pane, as follows:

```
<P>:resizep -D {amount}
```

If you're using the .tmux.conf file (covered in the previous chapter), then you'll already have a set of custom key bindings that make it easier to resize the *current* pane, as shown following:

- bind-key < resize-pane -L 5

- bind-key > resize-pane -R 5

- bind-key + resize-pane -U 5

- bind-key - resize-pane -D 5

Balancing

When creating a new split pane, tmux will try to keep them evenly balanced (i.e., of equal size), but after a while, you can find they shift out of balance. This can happen by chance but more often when you manually resize your panes to give more focus on a particular file.

For example, if you're doing test-driven development, you'll likely have two panes open: one holding your code under test, and the other displaying the results of your tests. Chances are, you want your test-results pane to be quite small and take up less space than the other pane holding the code being tested. To do this, you'll end up manually resizing the panes.

If you want to evenly distribute the space of yours panes (i.e., have them use an equal amount of space), use one of the following commands:

- <P>:select-layout even-horizontal

- <P>:select-layout even-vertical

▓ **Note** We saw the effect of these commands in the previous chapter, so please refer back to Figures 2-4 and 2-5.

Windows

In tmux, windows work in a similar way to how "tabs" work within your web browser. To create a new window, run the `<P>c` command (or `:new-window`, if you're using the command prompt).

You'll notice when creating a new window that tmux will automatically name it after the process that's running. For example, it will name the window `zsh`, as that binary is the default terminal shell running.

At any point, if you have to rename the current window, you can do this very simply, using the `<P>,` command. At this point, tmux will ask you to enter a new name for the window. If you're using the command prompt, the following example demonstrates the syntax structure:

```
:rename-window -t {window_id|window_name} {new_name}
```

Summary

In this chapter, we've covered the majority of the fundamental concepts that tmux is composed of. Let's take a quick look at what was covered so far.

- We discussed how tmux sessions work, such as how to create/ list/select/rename and attach/detach a session, as well as what benefits they provide.

- We then moved on to the concept of buffers and the screen viewport. I explained how overflowing content is displayed outside of the viewport and is still available within the current buffer, as well as how we can navigate the buffer, using tmux's copy mode.

- After that, we looked at how panes work and at their relationship to tmux windows, how we can create/manipulate and navigate panes, and how we can trigger a window or entire session to be closed, by removing all available panes.

- Finally, we covered the concept of tmux windows and how to create and rename them.

CHAPTER 3

Modifications

Using tmux "out of the box" is useful enough as it is, but most of the time, we'll want to make our lives a little easier, by adding some additional customizations (such as we did in Chapter 23, when we added custom configuration to our .tmux.conf file).

The modifications we'll be making this chapter aren't all strictly tmux configurations. For example, the following section contains modifications aimed at workarounds for reducing complexity and duplication through the use of shell alias' and functions. Other sections are aimed at further modifications to the .tmux.conf file itself.

The number of modifications you make will be down to what it is you're trying to simplify for yourself. For myself, I find I only require a small number of modifications that revolve around minor abstractions and fixing issues that I've stumbled across while using tmux.

Abstractions

There is a vast amount of tmux specific commands (each with varying options), which can be difficult to memorize. I find that the easiest way to resolve that particular problem is to abstract away the commands for something more palatable.

For example, I would find myself constantly having to look up the documentation for how to create named sessions, or attach to an existing session. No matter how often I would run those commands, I could not commit them to memory.

I decided that the simplest solution was to abstract the relevant commands that I found myself having the most difficulty with into some simple wrapper functions. These functions would be added into my .zshrc shell configuration file.

Note If you're not using the Zsh shell then simply add these to your .bashrc file or similar shell configuration file.

Most of the abstractions that I've created use standard shell functions; for others, I use a shell alias. Either way, you're free to use them or to modify them to suit your own needs, or even remove them completely and use the plain vanilla tmux commands, if you find this easier than working with abstractions.

Creating New Sessions

The first abstraction I made was to the command I probably use the most: creating a new "named" tmux session (as seen in the following code snippet):

```
function tmuxnew() {
  tmux new -s $1
}
```

Now this isn't necessarily a difficult command to remember, but if we're going to be abstracting other tmux commands, there is no harm in keeping things consistent. To execute this command, all I have to do is type tmuxnew {my_session_name} (you can shorten the name, if you prefer, to tn or tnew; whatever works for you) into my terminal shell, and if I forget to provide a name, the command will fail to run and remind me that I've not specified a session name.

But this in itself can be a bit long-winded, because we have to think up a unique name for each session we create. It would be better if we could create a new session that was named after the project directory in which we are currently residing. That's what the following alias does for us. We simply run tat, and it'll pick up the name of the current folder and use that, as in the following:

```
alias tat="tmux new-session -As $(basename $PWD | tr . -)"
```

The way it works is by utilizing the –A flag for the new-session command. The –A flag makes new-session behave like attach-session, if the specified session name already exists. From there, instead of hard-coding in a session name (which wouldn't be very useful), we use the shell's $() command substitution feature, which evaluates the commands specified within the parentheses before the main/containing command is run. The returned value from the subshell commands is what is used for the session name.

To get the folder name, we use the basename command and pass it the current working directory name ($PWD). So if $PWD returned /Users/markmcdonnell, the basename for that path would be markmcdonnell.

Finally, we pipe (|) the folder name through to the translate (tr) command, which converts any dots (.) into hyphens, to ensure the session name is valid. This avoids issues wherein the folder name is x.y.z, by converting it into a valid name, such as x-y-z, before passing it to the new-session command.

▓ **Note** This technique was pioneered by http://robots.thoughtbot.com/.

Attaching to Sessions

As you can probably imagine, there are similar abstractions that we can make at this point, such as the following code snippet, which indicates that I want to connect to a specific named session:

```
function tmuxopen() {
  tmux attach -t $1
}
```

Typically, I'll execute tmux ls to get a list of open sessions, and then once I have that list of sessions and I know what session names I have already, I can run tmuxopen {my_session_name} to reattach to the specified session.

Destroying Sessions

When I want to kill a specific session completely, I use the following function:

```
function tmuxkill() {
  tmux kill-session -t $1
}
```

For me, to use this function, I have to know the name of the session I want to kill, so I'll execute tmux ls first, to get a list of open sessions, and then once I have that list of sessions, I'll know which sessions I have already. Then I can run tmuxkill {my_session_name} to destroy the specified session. But what happens when we want to destroy *all* our tmux sessions?

▨ **Note**   In the following example, I will demonstrate a manual solution to the problem of destroying multiple tmux sessions at once, by using a collection of Unix commands. There is a simpler solution using tmux's built-in command tmux kill-server. The reasoning behind showing readers a more manual process is to encourage you to become more comfortable working from the command line and to take advantage of tools that can help you resolve issues for which there are no built-in commands.

OK, so we could execute the tmuxkill function multiple times, but that's just slow and very tedious. Instead, we can use some Unix wizardry to help make killing all our tmux sessions much easier:

```
alias tmuxkillall="tmux ls | cut -d : -f 1 | xargs
-I {} tmux kill-session -t {}"
```

This might seem long and confusing, but with a little background information on the individual commands, it can start to make a little more sense. I'm not going to get into the nitty-gritty of how each of the commands works, as this isn't a book about Unix, but I will try and break it down as simply as I can.

A top-level view of the alias shows us that we have three commands in place (tmux ls, cut, and xargs), and each command is separated by a pipe (|), which means the result from the previous command is passed through to the next command.

The tmux ls command displays into stdout (i.e., the terminal screen) a list of open tmux sessions that looks something like the following output, which highlights that I have three separate sessions running on my machine (one called my_session, another called work, and the last called side project):

```
my_session: 1 windows (created Thur Aug 28 17:01:34 2014) [118x32]
work: 4 windows (created Fri Aug 29 09:59:12 2014) [118x32]
side project: 2 windows (created Mon Aug 25 08:29:05 2014) [118x32]
```

From this output, we can see that the part we need is before the colon (:), as that is the session name. For us to be able to parse the session name from the output, we have to use the cut command. We tell the command to use the colon as a "field" delimiter (-d :), which means it'll split each line of output into chunks, using the colon as its indicator of where to make a split. Then we tell the command to return us the first chunk or field (-f 1).

Now that we have the session name, we pass that through to xargs to handle. We first tell xargs to hold the value we're passing to it, so we can reference it using the syntax {} (we do this via the -I {} flag). We then tell xargs what command we want it to execute (in this case, tmux kill-session -t {}), and where we typically would use the session name, we place a {}.

Because we've used the cut command (which processes multiple lines of data), each listed tmux session will be processed and parsed for its session name and passed to xargs to handle triggering the kill-session command.

Extending the Message Display Time

By default, tmux sets the length of time a message is displayed onscreen to 750 milliseconds. This is a remarkably short amount of time for you to decipher the message that's being highlighted to you by tmux. Typically, I'll misuse a tmux function, whereupon tmux will notify me of the correct syntax (or the error), by utilizing its own display-message command.

Inevitably, I always miss what the message said (or didn't get enough time to read the entire message, or the commands correct options), and so I have to resort to executing <P>~ to display all messages that have recently been sent, just so I can get a longer glimpse at the message I missed.

Instead of opening a list of old messages, a better solution is to extend the display message time, using the display-time command. Let's extend to two seconds the message display time for all currently open windows (using the -g flag), by adding the following setting to our .tmux.conf file:

```
set-option -g display-time 2000
```

Repeatable Keys

When creating your own key bindings, tmux provides an additional flag (-r), which lets you control how the key is repeated. In Chapter 1, I demonstrated a basic usage of the bind-key command's -r flag, but in this section, I want to cover another example of how it is useful. Specifically, I would like to demonstrate how this flag can help to improve tmux's ability to switch panes.

To begin, let's imagine we have two panes open horizontally next to each other. The left pane has a text document open in the Vim text editor, and the right pane (the currently focused pane) is a terminal shell. Now imagine we want to move to the left pane (which has Vim open) and then start moving the cursor to the right (while within Vim).

To do this, you would first execute <P><Left-Arrow> to move the cursor into the left tmux pane, and then once inside the left pane (and subsequently within Vim), you would press <Right-Arrow> to start navigating through the Vim buffer.

What you would typically find is that the cursor would not move to the right of the buffer (inside of Vim); instead, the cursor would move back to the right tmux pane. But why? The cause of this is to do with the use of tmux's default configuration and the -r flag when defining our custom key bindings.

A naive workaround to this problem would be to simply wait a fraction of a second before we pressed the <Right-Arrow> key. But a better solution is to prevent the problem altogether, by re-creating the default bindings ourselves to not use the -r flag, as shown in the following code sample:

```
bind-key Up    select-pane -U
bind-key Down  select-pane -D
bind-key Left  select-pane -L
bind-key Right select-pane -R
```

The -r flag indicates that the key binding can be "repeated." What this means in a practical sense is that when you execute the key binding, you can press another tmux binding key without having to include the prefix. This helps to chain lots of tmux commands together more efficiently.

Hence, when you execute the <P><Left-Arrow> (to move to the pane holding Vim), followed by <Right-Arrow> (which you'd expect to move the cursor within Vim to the right), it, in fact, moves the cursor back over to the right pane, as if you had pressed <P><Right-Arrow>.

Restoring Broken Commands

Along with adding your own abstractions and working around subtle nuisances in how tmux interacts with other programs, you may also notice some problems with your terminal shell environment.

For me, one of the biggest annoyances was that my bck-i-search command (which allows us to search iteratively back through our previous command history) stopped working while within tmux.

The reason for some of this was owing to my rebinding <C-r> to dynamically source the .tmux.conf file, whereas other machines I would be working on would have all kinds of different custom settings that could cause conflicts.

I found the easiest solution was to add the following snippets, which helped resolve these issues by redefining the key bindings to do exactly what I expected them to:

```
bindkey '^R' history-incremental-search-backward
bindkey '^A' beginning-of-line
bindkey '^E' end-of-line
```

Summary

This was a relatively short chapter, but I trust you found the topics covered interesting and helpful in resolving some practical concerns when using tmux in your day-to-day workflow. Let's have a quick recap.

- We started by looking at some abstractions for creating and attaching to new sessions and automating the session naming process by utilizing some basic Unix commands to parse out the current folder name.

- Similarly, we looked at how we can kill individual sessions and, again using some basic Unix scripting, kill all open tmux sessions.

- We looked at how best to resolve an issue of the short amount of time a message is displayed onscreen, using the display-time command.

- We moved on to resolving an issue with the default tmux configuration, whereby interacting with Vim was made problematic, due to the bind-key and its -r repeat flag.

- Finally, we looked at resolving issues with standard terminal commands that break once executed in the terminal, within a tmux session.

CHAPTER 4

Copy and Paste

One of the most arduous tasks within tmux is the need to be able to copy and paste content from a buffer. The problem isn't so much copying content from our buffer (although that isn't the simplest of tasks, as we'll see in the first few sections of this chapter), but more so that there is no native capability to paste content that has been copied from a tmux buffer into other external programs.

In this chapter, we'll look at how copy and paste works in general (for all platforms) and then review some workarounds for the issue of copying content from tmux into another program for both Mac and Linux.

Note Some of the solutions provided in this chapter are dependent on the use of tmux 1.8+.

Copy Mode

In tmux, all content is placed inside a buffer, and if there is not enough screen space to hold all of the buffer content, it will effectively be scrolled "off screen." So for us to be able to go back and view the offscreen buffer content, we first have to get tmux into "copy mode."

I briefly covered copy mode in Chapter 2, but just to quickly recap: to enter copy mode, either execute the key binding <P>[or the command <P>:copy-mode, which routes through tmux's command prompt.

Once you're inside copy mode, you can navigate around, using the arrow keys and quit copy mode, by pressing either q or <Enter> when you're done.

Note The Linux keys to quit copy mode are <Esc> and q but not <Enter>.

For us to begin making a selection of text, we'll have to press <Space>, and this will result in the text being highlighted as we start navigating around with the arrow keys. To copy our selection, we have to press <Enter> for the selection to be placed into tmux's "paste buffer" (space in memory).

▓ **Note**   The Linux key for selection is <C-Space>, and the key to copy the selection to the paste buffer is <Esc-w> (or, more accurately, whatever your "modifier" key is set to on your keyboard: <M-w>).

Paste Buffer

Once you have content in the paste buffer, you can then paste it into any other tmux buffer you have open, which includes buffers that are open within a completely different tmux session (see Figure 4-1)!

Figure 4-1. *Example of tmux's paste buffer*

The paste buffer keeps a history of all copied content, so you can copy multiple items and then keep track of them within the paste buffer. To list the current items stored within the paste buffer, you can either execute the key binding <P># or the command <P>:list-buffers, which routes through tmux's command prompt.

Each item in the paste buffer is numbered, so you can easily identify the order in which items were added (newest items are placed at the top). To close the list-buffers screen, either press q or <Enter> (or q and <Esc>, if you're a Linux user). If you would instead like to see the full content of the latest buffer, there is a shortcut command that does that and is run via the command prompt <P>:show-buffer.

The show-buffer screen is only a temporary visual aid. The content is not taken out of the paste buffer, and it is not placed inside your current buffer. If you would like to paste the latest item within the paste buffer into your current buffer, you can use the <P>] key binding or the command <P>:paste-buffer, which routes through tmux's command prompt.

You can also capture the current pane in its entirety, using the command <P>:capture-pane, and from there, you can even save the latest paste buffer directly into a file, if you want, using the command <P>:save-buffer ~/Desktop/foo.txt. (See Figure 4-2).

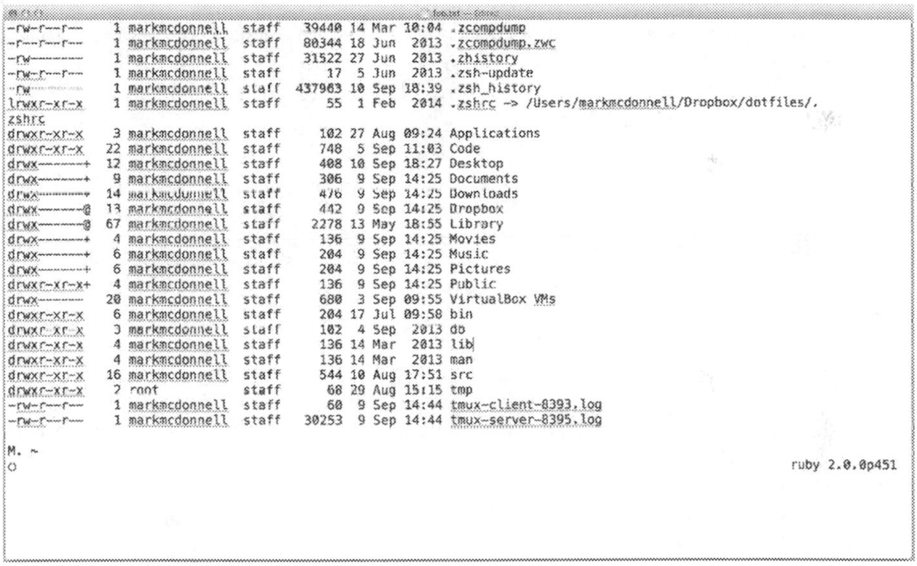

Figure 4-2. *Output from capturing a pane and saving it to a file*

If you have lots of items within your paste buffer and you need a specific item to paste into your current buffer, you can select the item you require by executing either the key binding <P>= or the command <P>:choose-buffer, which routes through tmux's command prompt. For example, you could open the Vim text editor within your current buffer and then run <P>=, to begin navigating the list of items within the paste buffer, and then select one to have its content pasted directly into Vim.

▓ **Note**   If you're using the .tmux.conf configuration provided in Chapter 1, then be aware that the default tmux command <P>= (which maps to <P>:choose-buffer) has been overridden. So you'll either want to remove the custom key binding the configuration file assigns to <P>=, or use the long form <P>:choose-buffer.

Pasting Between Programs

The problem that confuses most tmux users is the inability to paste what has been copied from the tmux paste buffer into a different program (because the paste buffer is not the same thing as the operating system's clipboard). We'll take a look at how to resolve this in both the Mac and Linux operating systems.

Plug-in Solution

Before I jump into the manual process, there is a more automated solution, involving installing a tmux plug-in called tmux-yank (`https://github.com/tmux-plugins/tmux-yank`), which works for both Mac AND Linux operating systems and is very simple to install by either following the manual installation steps or using a tmux plug-in manager (`https://github.com/tmux-plugins/tpm`).

Mac OS X

If you're using Mac OS X as your development environment, the solution involves the installation of a program called `reattach-to-user-namespace` and a modification to your `.tmux.conf` file.

The tmux program running on Mac OS X has issues accessing the namespace it originates from, meaning tmux requires an additional program to reattach it to that namespace. This is a bug that Apple fixed for the popular multiplexer Screen (`www.gnu.org/software/screen/`), but the patch isn't possible to apply to tmux, owing to private undocumented functions being utilized by Apple. This means we have to implement our solution.

First, to install the `reattach-to-user-namespace` program, you can either manually compile it, by following instructions from its online repository here: `https://github.com/ChrisJohnsen/tmux-MacOSX-pasteboard`, or you can take the easier route and install it using the Homebrew package manager, which can be downloaded by following the current instructions found at `http://brew.sh/`.

```
brew install reattach-to-user-namespace
```

The following code snippet demonstrates the changes we have to make to our `.tmux.conf` file to configure tmux correctly:

```
set -g default-command "reattach-to-user-namespace -l '/bin/zsh'"
bind-key -t vi-copy 'v' begin-selection bind-key -t vi-copy 'y' copy-pipe
"reattach-to-user-namespace pbcopy"
```

Effectively, we've instructed tmux to use the wrapper program (`reattach-to-user-namespace`) as the default command that should be run when a new tmux window is created. The specified program then wraps around the Zsh shell.

The other two key bindings will make tmux more like Vim (i.e., more familiar and easier to work with), by implementing similar key bindings for making a selection and yanking content from the buffer. Once you have this modification, you will be able to enter copy mode and simply hit v to begin making a selection of the buffer and then, when ready to copy, press y to yank.

▓ **Note**   For a complete breakdown of why the access to system clipboard is broken on Mac OS X, and to understand how the solution works (including implementation details of the reattach-to-user-namespace program), I highly recommend having a read through the GitHub repo https://github.com/ChrisJohnsen/tmux-MacOSX-pasteboard, which covers all of this in painstaking detail.

Linux

If you're using Linux, you'll have to make sure you have xclip installed first. Depending on your distribution, the installation can be done using either a yum install xclip or apt-get install xclip, so pick what's relevant to you.

Once xclip is installed, you should simply have to add the following changes to your .tmux.conf file:

```
bind-key -t vi-copy 'v' begin-selection
bind-key -t vi-copy 'y' copy-pipe "xclip"
```

▓ **Note**   Depending on your distribution, the bindings may have to be modified to suit. For example, we can also use an alternative method of tmux save-buffer - | xclip -i -sel clipboard to copy content, and tmux set-buffer \"$(xclip -o -sel clipboard)\"; tmux paste-buffer to paste.

Working from a VM

If you're running Linux within a virtual machine (VM) from the Mac operating system (using VirtualBox, VMWare, or some other virtualization software, in addition to something such as Vagrant to manage the setup/tear-down of VMs), you'll find that the preceding solution doesn't work. This is because you're running a GUI-less version of Linux that has no concept of a system clipboard.

The clipboard programs you can install on Linux are typically developed to work using a system known as X-Windows. So even if you install something like xclip on your Linux VM, you'll still have issues getting the preceding tmux configurations to send tmux selections to the xclip program (as a terminal-only version of Linux inside a VM won't have the required X-Windows dependencies).

If you're using Vagrant to start and manage your VMs, then the solution to this problem is quite simple. First, you'll have to install and run the software XQuartz (`http://xquartz.macosforge.org/`, which is a Mac OS equivalent of the X-Windows system). Second, you'll have to modify your `Vagrantfile` to include the following option, so that when you start up your VM, Vagrant can forward the XQuartz program onto the VM to use (meaning `xclip` will start working):

```
config.ssh.forward_x11 = true
```

Finally, you'll want to modify the `.tmux.conf` setting, so it looks like the following snippet:

```
bind-key -t vi-copy 'v' begin-selection
bind-key -t vi-copy 'y' copy-pipe "xclip -selection clipboard"
```

Summary

Let's take a moment to summarize some of things you've learned over the course of this chapter.

- We discussed the fundamental issue of copying and pasting with tmux across different programs, along with some complexity with the commands required to select and copy specific portions of tmux's screen buffer.

- We first took a look at tmux's copy mode and what its purpose is (which is to allow us to scroll back through content that wasn't possible to fix in the screen's viewport). You also learned the different commands and key bindings that help us navigate through copy mode (and the variations between Mac and Linux).

- Then we moved on to reviewing tmux's paste buffer, how content is stored in the paste buffer, and how you might retrieve content, using specific key bindings or more granular control with commands such as `:choose-buffer`. (You also discovered how to copy an entire pane's content using the `:capture-pane` command.)

- Finally, we looked at a quick solution for ensuring we're able to properly copy and paste from tmux into different unrelated programs, as well as how to make the process easier, by utilizing some key bindings that make tmux behave more like Vim.

CHAPTER 5

Pane/Window Management

Being able to efficiently manage your tmux windows and panes is a skill that usually is acquired over a long period of time, as you find yourself becoming more comfortable with this powerful screen-management tool.

In this chapter, I'm going to review some key binding shortcuts and offer up some tips that will, I hope, help you become much more proficient in your daily workflow. We'll begin by looking at how we can better manage tmux panes and then look at some of the tmux window features available.

Pane Management

You'll find that a common process in tmux is creating lots of windows (as well as creating multiple panes within those windows) for handling the different aspects of individual tasks. The number of windows and panes you open is dependent on the type of work you do and the user in general, but regardless of background, the following tips will help you keep control.

Moving Between Two Commonly Used Panes

Imagine that you have four panes open in a grid format (i.e., two panes in one row and two panes below in a second row), as the following diagram indicates:

```
---------------------
|   A   |   B   |
---------------------
|   C   |   D   |
---------------------
```

If your cursor were currently focused inside the A pane, and you wanted to get to the D pane, the quickest route to doing so would be to use the display-panes command (or the key binding <P>q).

But this is always a mental hurdle to jump over when you're trying to work quickly and are bouncing back and forth between specific panes, i.e., moving back and forth between the panes A and D.

In these scenarios, I personally find the last-pane command (or, more specifically, the key binding <P>;) to be a much more efficient way of moving back and forth between two commonly used panes.

Full-Screen Current Pane

This is one of the most useful features of tmux panes, because it helps to keep other content hidden. The typical use case I have for this is when I have two panes open, one running Vim and the other my terminal shell that's watching some code files for changes and then displaying the results of my code's suite of unit tests.

In this scenario, I'll usually move my cursor's focus into the pane containing Vim and run <P>z (or the long form command, <P>:resize-pane -Z) to cause the pane to fill the window (subsequently hiding the other pane I have open), so I can work primarily on my code.

From there, I'll continue working as normal, and if there is ever a point at which I have to refer to my terminal to check my test suite output, I simply move into the other pane, which triggers the full-screen mode to stop (or I would execute the same <P>z key binding again to revert back).

Break a Pane Out into a Separate Window

Sometimes, a pane can start to contain so much content or process output that you wish you had more room for it. In most cases, you can use the previous tip of going full-screen with <P>z, but depending on the context, you might be more comfortable just moving the content to a new window.

Luckily for us, tmux has a built-in command that handles that exact issue; it's the break-pane command, and it has a nice key binding shortcut <P>!

Convert a Window into a Pane (Within Another Window)

In the previous example, we broke a pane out of a window, so it became its own self-contained window. In this section, we want to do the reverse behavior, which can be achieved using tmux's join-pane command, like so:

```
<P>:join-pane -s {source_window} -t {target_window}
```

In the preceding example, we tell tmux to join the source window into the target window. This will remove the source window as a separate window and convert it into a new pane within the target window.

Rotate Panes Within Current Window

When you have multiple panes open, it can be useful to rotate them, so that you have one pane aligned next to another relevant pane (maybe to make some comparisons of data easier).

In Figure 5-1 (following), we can see that we have four panes open. In the top left, we're running htop (http://hisham.hm/htop/); in the top right pane, we're running vtop (http://parall.ax/vtop); within the bottom right pane, we're running the standard/ ubiquitous top command; and within the bottom left pane, we have an empty terminal pane not running anything.

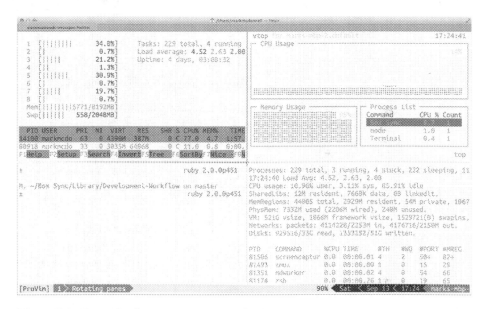

Figure 5-1. *Example of some processes running in separate panes*

If we decided that we wanted to have the bottom-right pane (top) placed in the top-left position (so that it was placed to the left of the top-right pane currently holding the vtop process), we would run either the <P>} key binding (to rotate the pane clockwise) or the <P>{ key binding (to rotate the pane counterclockwise).

In this example, it wouldn't matter which pane we currently were focused on. We would just execute the relevant command until the panes were positioned exactly how we needed them to be.

Changing Pane Layouts

There are built-in algorithms that tmux uses to provide a different layout when triggering the <P><Space> key binding. This binding can be executed multiple times and will cause the layout of the panes to change, whereby you can stop whenever you find a layout that suits your current working environment.

Synchronizing Pane Input

Imagine that you have a group of panes open, and for each pane, you are SSH'ed into a different remote server (for which you're tailing some system log file). If you wanted to execute the same set of commands for each of the processes running on each of the servers, then instead of doing this manually (i.e., executing the command in the current pane and moving to the next pane and repeat), we can automate this slightly.

To do this, we have to instruct tmux to synchronize each open pane, using the command `<P>:setw synchronize-panes`, so that any input entered into any one of the panes will be replicated across all of them.

▓ **Note** By default, the command toggles the behavior, but you can specify an `on` or `off` status as well (for the purpose of automation via shell scripts), for example, `:setw synchronize-panes off`.

Window Management

Unlike panes, windows aren't as much of a large management concern. There are also a limited number of use cases for handling windows. Once created, you'll either want to navigate them, close them, move them, or swap them around. Let's take a look at each of these suggestions.

Navigating Windows

There are a couple of ways to navigate through windows: manually (using key bindings) and via a visual list. Let's review both of these options . . .

Manually

To navigate manually, you again have a few options available to you: sequential or indirect. When navigating sequentially, we can use the key bindings `<P>n` (to move to the next window) or `<P>p` (to move to the previous window). When navigating indirectly, we can use the key binding `<P>{n}`, whereby you'll replace {n} with the numerical index of the window.

Visual List

We can have tmux display a list of the available windows for us and then use our arrow keys to navigate the list. We display the list, using the `<P>w` key binding or via the `choose-window` command (see Figure 5-2 for an example).

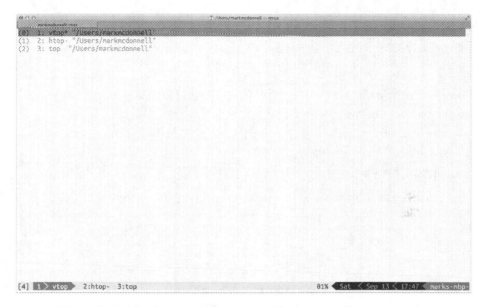

Figure 5-2. *Output of the choose-window command*

When you have used your arrow keys to highlight the window you wish to access, simply press <CR> to jump to the relevant window.

Closing Windows

There are three ways to close a window, as follows:

1. Immediate key binding

2. Command-line prompt

3. Confirmation prompt key binding

Immediate

Most of the time, I'll use the <C-d> key binding, which sends an EOF (http://en.wikipedia.org/wiki/End-of-file) signal to the terminal process, causing it to instantly terminate.

Command-Line Mode

The `kill-window` command will immediately close the current window.

▦ **Note**   You can pass the `-a` flag, which will mean *all* windows will be closed, except the current window or the window specified using the target `-t` flag.

Confirmation Prompt

The `<P>&` key binding is an abstraction around the `kill-window` command. It utilizes tmux's `confirm-before` feature (see the following Note) to ensure that a message is displayed within the command-line prompt, asking you to confirm whether you are sure you want to close the window.

▦ **Note**   By default, the `confirm-before` command will display a generic message constructed from the original command being executed. This message can be modified using the `confirm-before`'s `-p` flag. You can find more information in the tmux manual.

Finding Windows by Search Phrase

If you want to find a window by either its identifier (i.e., the name you gave the window) or by its contents, the `<P>f` key binding might be what you're after. You can also use the `find-window` command itself.

Moving and Switching Windows Within the Current Session

Thanks to tmux's client-server architecture, we have the extraordinary power to move a window not only between a single session but also between completely different sessions, using the `move-window` command. Let's see a simple example first, in which we move the window into another position within the current session.

Imagine that we have three windows open (indexed 1, 2, and 3), and we want to move window 1 to the end of the list. To do this would require running the following command:

```
<P>:move-window -t 4
```

You can see in the preceding example that we specify an index that isn't already taken and is higher than any defined (in this case, 4). This works by using the target (`-t`) flag to specify what index we want to move the window to.

Similarly, we can swap two windows. Using the same example as previously (three windows, indexed 1, 2, and 3), imagine that we wanted to swap windows 1 and 3. To do this, we would run the following command:

```
<P>:swap-window -s 1 -t 3
```

In the preceding example, we've used the swap-window command, along with the source flag (-s), indicating the window we want to swap and the target flag (-t) to indicate the alternate window it should be swapped with.

Moving Windows Between Different Sessions

It can be useful to reduce a complicated multi-window group of sessions down to a single session. In order to do this, you would have to decide what windows from each session you wanted to keep and somehow move them into another session that was to act as your consolidated session.

To achieve this result, we could use the <P>. key binding (or the long-form move-window -t {session:window_id} command). When you run <P>, tmux will ask you to choose a window. This means you will have to enter the name of the session you want to move the window into.

You can also specify a specific window index that you want it to move to. For example, foo:2 would move the window to the foo session and position the window into index 2. If you were to specify a numeric session identifier that wasn't recognized, the window would be moved to that index within the current session.

We don't even have to be in a specific session to be able to move a window into another session. In the following example, we use the "source" flag (-s) to indicate that we want the index 1 window within the foo session to be moved into the bar session.

```
tmux move-window -s foo:1 -t bar
```

▓ **Note**   If the current window has the same name as the session you're moving it into, the move will fail, as tmux will get confused and think you're trying to move the window back into itself.

Sharing Windows Between Sessions

You may find that, rather than moving a window to another session, you wish you could just share it. This is possible by using tmux's link-window command. Imagine that we have two tmux sessions, foo and bar, both having one window each. The foo session's window is named fwin, and the bar session's window is named bwin.

If we were currently inside the foo session, and we decided that we wanted to share the fwin window with the bar session, we would simply have to execute the command as follows: <P>:link-window -t bar:2.

Note, in the preceding command, that we don't specify a source. This is because we're inside the foo session. If we were not, we would have used the -s flag to identify the source session/window.

Now, any changes that are made to the fwin window, whether it be inside the foo session or the bar session, will be reflected in the other session. But be careful, as closing the window in one session will close it in any other session it is shared with.

▦ **Note** Sometimes when sharing a window, you might hit upon a conflict, whereby the destination session already has a window with the same identifier. To resolve this problem, you can choose to "kill" the window in the destination session, by adding the -k flag to the command.

Summary

You've learned some important shortcuts in this chapter. These techniques can not only make you more proficient with multitasking across many different sessions but also give you more tools to extend the automation side of your tmux working environment. Let's quickly recap what was covered.

We started by looking at some of the different techniques for manipulating and managing tmux panes, such as how to move back and forth between two common panes, converting the current pane into full-screen mode to allow us to take advantage of the extra space, converting a window into a pane and changing the layout of panes within a single window, and synchronizing the input for multiple panes.

Finally, we began to review the options available for manipulating and managing tmux windows. This included considering multiple ways to navigate through windows, using key bindings or a more traditional visual list; closing windows, using either key bindings, command-line prompt, or an extra abstraction layer that incorporates the confirm-before command; filtering a list of windows, using a search pattern; and moving windows between either the current session or even external sessions, as well as how to share windows between multiple sessions.

CHAPTER 6

Scripting and Automation

In this chapter, we'll review some different built-in tmux commands that allow us to control to a very granular level how existing tmux sessions look and function, as well as modifying the boot-up process to open multiple sessions and to construct complex environment layouts within those sessions.

We'll also be taking a look at three variations of this process. The first will demonstrate both simple and advanced ways to instruct tmux what to open and how.

The second example will demonstrate how to run shell commands without triggering a new window to be generated, whereas the third example will return to a similar concept, as shown in the first example, but this time, utilizing a very popular open source alternative called tmuxinator.

Finally, I'll make mention of some additional tmux programs related to restoring and attaching existing processes.

Example 1: Automation

Following, we'll first examine a basic example, to give you an idea of how we can automate tmux to construct a specific layout. After that, we'll look at a slightly more complex example, to help demonstrate how we can chain together different tmux commands to give us total control of the layout and content of a tmux session.

Simple Example

To get us started with our simple demonstration of how to construct layouts programmatically, let's first put together a set of basic requirements.

1. Instruct tmux to connect to the last active session.

2. Access the first window open within that session.

3. Open the Vim text editor (*and* drop us into Vim's INSERT mode).

The command we need to actually fulfill these requirements is very simple and looks like the following:

```
tmux send-keys -t 1 "vim" "C-m" "i" "programmatic content here"
```

In the preceding example, we're executing the send-keys command from outside tmux, to indicate that this could well be dropped into an automated shell script, but it's fine to execute this via the tmux command prompt. The send-keys command requires us to specify a target (-t), and all the arguments that follow the target are "keys" to be sent to that target and executed sequentially.

So, in this case, we tell it to connect to pane one, but pane one of what? How does tmux know what session to connect to? In this instance, it uses the last active session we were connected to. Next, we pass the string "vim", followed by the string "C-m", which triggers Vim to open (this is effectively another way of describing the <Enter> key).

Finally, we execute "i" (which, if that key were pressed when Vim was open, would drop us into INSERT mode), followed by "programmatic content here", which, if you're playing along at home, you'll notice is entered into the current Vim buffer for us.

Targeting Specific Sessions

As we saw previously, we can target a pane in the latest session and control it with any command we wish to send to it. But we can also specify a *specific* session we want to target, as follows:

```
tmux send-keys -t foo:2 "vim" "C-m"
```

In the preceding example, we're telling tmux to open Vim and to specifically target (-t) the foo session and the second pane within that session (:2).

Advanced

Now that we've seen some basic sample usage, let's use some more tmux commands and string them together to build up a complex automated layout.

What we want to do in this example is automate the creation of a new session. In this session, we want two windows. The first window should show us the result of the top command. The second window should have Vim open and entered into INSERT mode. Let's consider what this automation looks like.

```
tmux new -s foo -d "top" && \
tmux split-window -t foo:1 && \
tmux break-pane && \
tmux send-keys "vim" "C-m" "i"
```

In the preceding example, we're executing a long list of commands (using the logical && operator to run them sequentially) across multiple lines (by using the backslash character, \), but we could very well place this command inside of a single line of a shell script and execute it that way. Let's now break down the preceding command, so that we can better understand what it's doing.

- `tmux new -s foo -d "top"`: We create a new session named foo and detach it (e.g., we don't jump into tmux; we stay at the terminal, and we tell tmux to run the `top` command inside the first window of that detached session).

- `tmux split-window -t foo:1`: We tell tmux to split the first window inside the `foo` session. (This creates two panes in the first window: the first pane holds the results of our `top` command, and the second pane is empty and holds our cursor's focus.)

- `tmux break-pane`: In the previous command, we targeted the `foo` session, so we won't have to tell tmux to target it again when we execute the `break-pane` command. Now, we tell tmux to break the current pane into its own window (this means the empty pane we created earlier is now its own window).

- `tmux send-keys "vim" "C-m" "i"`: tmux's current focus is the new window we just made via the `break-pane` command, and so from here, we tell tmux to open up Vim and enter INSERT mode (we saw this in our earlier "simple" example).

Example 2: Shell Commands

tmux provides a feature called `run-shell` that (as the name suggests) lets you run shell commands within tmux, but crucially, it doesn't create a new window for the results to be displayed in. Instead, the results are displayed temporarily within "copy mode" of the current (or specified) buffer.

Let's see the syntax structure of the command, and then we'll take a quick look at an example of how we can use it.

`<P>:run-shell [-b] [-t {pane_id}] "{shell_command}"`

In the preceding syntax structure, we can see that the tmux command accepts a `-b` flag, which allows us to run the shell command as a background process. This is useful because, if it's a long-running process, we don't want to be blocked by it. We can also instruct tmux to display the result of the command within a target pane of our choice, using the `-t` flag. Finally, we have the command itself we want to execute.

■ **Note**   The `-b` and `-t` flags are optional. If you don't specify a target pane, the current pane is used.

Once you run this command, the result of the shell command is displayed within tmux in copy mode, allowing you to scroll through the buffer. The `run-shell` command can be useful in situations in which we want to bind multiple commands to a single key binding. For example:

```
bind-key e select-pane -L \; run-shell "ls -la && ls ~/Desktop"
```

In the preceding example, we bind multiple tmux commands to the e key (we've bound the `select-pane` and `run-shell` commands), and that single key binding (when executed) will attempt to select the next pane to its left and then run the `ls -la && ls ~/Desktop` command, displaying the results within that pane's copy mode.

This command can also be useful for automating tmux via external scripts. For example, if you have an existing session open with two windows, you could script tmux at some point in time to execute a shell command to target the results into one of the panes within that session.

Conditional Key Bindings

There is a powerful and dynamic feature in tmux that lets you test your environment and bind a different set of commands to a custom key binding, depending on the result of your test.

As an example, the following code snippet uses tmux's `if-shell` command to first check if the folder Dropbox exists. If the value returned from the test is greater than zero, that means the folder exists, and we'll see the message "Folder exists" displayed. Otherwise, if the folder doesn't exist, we'll see the message "Folder does not exist."

```
bind-key u if-shell "test $(ls | grep Dropbox | wc -l) -gt 0"
"display-message 'Folder does not exist'" "display-message 'Folder exists'"
```

What this ultimately means is that you can cater your tmux key bindings to suit the environment it is running in. For example, in Chapter 4, we looked at binding a different command, based on whether you were running on a Linux platform. We could have used the `if-shell` function to dynamically bind the value, depending on whether the xclip function was available or not. (I didn't do that, as there was other functionality that was specific to Linux that required modification.)

Example 3: tmuxinator

Remember our first example where we wrote a script to automate the construction of different layouts for us? Well, there is a Ruby-based project called tmuxinator (https://github.com/tmuxinator/tmuxinator) that simplifies the script-writing process, by allowing us to trade our shell script for a YAML configuration file.

You can install tmuxinator by using the following command: `gem install tmuxinator`. To create a new project is as simple as running the following command:

```
tmuxinator new {project}
```

After running the preceding command, you should notice that a .tmuxinator folder has been created in your user's $HOME directory, and inside that folder will be a YAML file named after your project.

For example, if the command you executed was tmuxinator new foobar, you should see the following folder structure within the directory in which you ran that command:

```
.
├── .tmuxinator
│       └── foobar.yaml
│
```

The content of the YAML file will look something like the following (these are the default settings, which you'll want to change to suit your own project requirements):

```
name: foobar
root: ~/your_directory
windows:
  - editor:
      layout: main-vertical
      panes:
        - vim
        - guard
  - server: bundle exec rails s
  - logs: tail -f log/development.log
```

In the preceding YAML file, you'll see that the windows key defines different windows you want to have open when you run the project. You can see that, by default, if you specify a window key, the value is a command that tmux can run. In the preceding example, we have a server window that tells tmux to run the bundle exec rails s command (which starts up a web server for a Ruby on Rails–based project), and the logs window runs the tail -f log/development.log command, which displays information from a specific log file on our file system.

The editor window is a little bit more interesting, as it gives us more control over the layout of our editor window. In the preceding example, we can see we've defined a layout we want to use (in this case, main-vertical), along with a set of panes we want the window to contain, and what commands to run within those panes (in this case, execute the vim and guard commands).

Now, whenever we want to run our project, we use the following command:

```
tmuxinator start {project_name}
```

Depending on your requirements and experience writing your own provisioning shell scripts, you might find tmuxinator is a welcome addition to your toolset and that the configuration format works better for you than rolling your own tmux-focused shell scripts.

Restoration

There are two areas of tmux that have (up until recently) been problematic and have gone unresolved, but we'll take a look at some potential workarounds that could be the first steps toward finally finding a resolution. They are:

1. Attaching an existing process to a new tmux session

2. Restoring state upon a system restart

Attaching Processes

The first issue is one that can (at the time of writing) only be resolved for the Linux environment by installing a binary called Reptyr (`https://github.com/nelhage/reptyr`), using your package manager of choice. For example, either `yum install reptyr` or `apt-get install reptyr` should do the trick.

The reason this solution is Linux-only is because Mac OS X and other Unix environments don't support the `ptrace` shell command (among other required Linux-based system architecture). Although this restriction might not be such a big deal if you mainly use a Mac for GUI-based work and a virtual machine (e.g., tools such as VirtualBox and VMWare alongside Vagrant and Docker) for your development environment.

The usage process itself is pretty simple.

- First you make your process a background process (i.e. `<C-z>`).

- Disown the process from its parent (e.g., `disown {process_name}`).

- Start your multiplexer (e.g., `tmux`).

- Attach process (e.g., `reptyr $(pgrep {process_name})` or `reptyr {pid}`).

▓ **Note**   Reptyr can work with other multiplexers (e.g., screen).

Restoring State

The problem of restoring state, when your operating system restarts, is a tricky one, because there is only so much that can be done to record the data you were working with and the state it was in at the point of shutting down.

Luckily, there is a tmux plug-in called tmux-resurrect (`https://github.com/tmux-plugins/tmux-resurrect`), which solves this exact problem and will go to great lengths to restore all of the following items:

- All sessions, windows, panes, and their relevant order

- The current working directory for each tmux pane

- Exact pane layouts within tmux windows

- Active and alternative sessions

- Active and alternative windows for each session

- The tmux windows that have focus

- The active pane for each tmux window

- Programs running within a tmux pane

- Restoration of Vim sessions (this is optional)

▓ **Note** The author of the tmux-resurrect plug-in also provides a tmux plug-in manager (https://github.com/tmux-plugins/tpm), which makes installing tmux add-ons and plug-ins much easier.

Summary

In this chapter, I've covered some very important and fundamental functionality of tmux, which allows us to control the way tmux works and, if used in the right situations, can help to automate the entire process of bootstrapping your working environment. Let's take a moment to review what you've learned.

- First, I demonstrated how to programmatically control tmux, using the send-keys, split-window and break-pane commands (including how to target specific sessions).

- We then saw how to execute shell commands and review the results within the current pane. (You now know that we can also direct the output of any shell command into any tmux pane of our choosing, by using the -t flag.) You also learned how to conditionally bind a key command, based on some dynamic equation.

- We also examined the popular tmuxinator Ruby program, which helps to automate complex layouts via a simple YAML configuration file.

- Finally, we reviewed some potential workarounds to traditionally complex problems related to restoring state within tmux (caused by a system restart) and also how to attach an already running process to a tmux session.

CHAPTER 7

■ ■ ■

Pair Programming

When using tmux, we sometimes forget how powerful the client/server model that it implements is. For example, we all know that because of the client/server model, we can create multiple sessions on a single server and then at any point, we can jump between sessions, as we are able to connect to any session on the tmux server that we have running in the background.

But who's to say that the server has to be running on *our* machine! This is where this chapter steps in, to help demonstrate how you can utilize tmux to benefit users who are pair programming.

If you've not heard the term before, *pair programming* is the process of two developers sitting around a single computer and working together to solve the problem they've been presented with. The process takes the form of one developer typing code, while the other developer helps keep the thought process flowing (e.g., they aren't just sitting around twiddling their thumbs, waiting to jump on the keyboard). After a few hours, the pair will swap positions, allowing the other person to take a different mindset and approach to the problem they are solving.

As you can imagine, this is typically done in a single location (i.e., both developers are in the same room, sitting at the same computer), but what happens if you have to pair program with a colleague who works remotely? Well, this is where using tmux can help, but before I dive into the details of how this works, I would like first to present you with a one-line solution . . .

The Simple Route

I would argue that the easiest way to pair program with a colleague is by using the free service http://tmate.io/, which allows you to install their software tmate onto your computer and thus share your computer with a remote colleague.

To install the software, please refer to the web site for instructions (tmate is available for both Mac OS X and Linux distributions). Once installed, you can execute the single command tmate, which first utilizes a modified version of tmux (so you'll notice that it will pick up your local .tmux.conf configuration file), and once started, will display an ssh command for you to provide to your colleague, allowing him/her access to your computer. The ssh command will look something like the following: ssh abcd1XOfrvh1egxSysQYa1GIz@am.tmate.io.

Once your colleague has connected to the session, you'll see a small message at the foot of the tmate program, indicating that a user has joined the session: Your mate has joined the session (212.58.231.91).

From here, you can do most things you can do using standard tmux (although there are *some* commands that won't work, such as moving a window). It's important to remember that the user who has connected to the tmate session now has complete control over your computer, and so that user could effectively rm -rf / and wipe your computer clean (or install any kind of software when you weren't looking), so take care to whom you give the ssh command.

I would almost always recommend this as your go-to solution, as it's super-simple to set up, compared to doing things manually yourself (which we'll see in the next section).

The Custom Route

There are multiple ways to pair program using tmux. In the preceding section, we used a simple predefined route that automates some of what we will be looking at within this section. For example, we could open ssh access on our own computer, which would allow another user to connect directly to our machine. Alternatively, we could install tmux on a remote server and have both users connect to that single server, and, again, from there, we would have a few different options available to us.

Each option presents different pros and cons, and I'll aim to demonstrate each one, so that you can choose for yourself which is the most appropriate. I want to state upfront that I don't have the luxury of a dedicated server, and I'm far too cheap to spend even a few pennies spinning up some Amazon EC2 instances (although they are very cheap). So, instead of having a real server, I'll use Vagrant (www.vagrantup.com) to set up these examples and use it to mimic different user logins.

▓ **Note**   Vagrant is a tool for making the creation of virtual machines quick and easy. I'll cover it in more detail in the next chapter, but for now, I'll cover just enough to carry out the examples.

Vagrant Setup

To get started with Vagrant, first download it from www.vagrantup.com and install it. Vagrant has a hard dependency on a virtualization program, such as VirtualBox, which can be downloaded from www.virtualbox.org. Once you have both installed, you're ready for the next step.

Vagrant is a command line–based tool, and it works by reading configuration settings from a file called a Vagrantfile. The following code snippet shows the content of the Vagrantfile required to bring up an instance of a Linux Ubuntu instance:

```
VAGRANTFILE_API_VERSION = "2"
Rosary
Vagrant.configure(VAGRANTFILE_API_VERSION) do |config|
  config.vm.box = "ubuntu/trusty64"
end
```

You'll probably have noticed that the configuration is written using Ruby programming and that it's also quite a small file (there are many configuration settings available, but for our purposes, this is all we need).

To bring up our Linux Ubuntu instance, we simply run the following command vagrant up, (you'll need to run this command from the same location as your Vagrantfile) which will then send a stream of output to our terminal screen, informing us that Vagrant is spinning up a new Ubuntu instance for us. Once the instance is successfully brought up, you can log in to the VM (virtual machine) by running the command vagrant ssh.

▓ **Note**　Vagrant works with multiple virtualization programs. The main two are VirtualBox and VMWare. If you have more than one of them installed (and VirtualBox is not the default), the vagrant up command will require an additional flag that indicates the provider to use, for example, --provider=virtualbox or --provider=vmware_fusion.

Share Session via Single-User Account

In the following steps, we'll be creating a single user on our VM (if you're applying this to a real-world situation, this would be a case of you creating a new user on a remote server), which means two individual users can then log in to the VM, using this new single/shared account. Once the first user is logged in, he or she will create a new tmux session.

- Log in to the VM:

  vagrant ssh

- Switch to root user (so you can add new users):

  su

- Create new user foo:

  adduser foo

- Close connection to the VM:

  ```
  exit
  ```

- Reconnect to the VM using the new foo user:

  ```
  ssh -i $(vagrant ssh-config | grep IdentityFile | awk
  '{print $2}') -l foo -p 2222 -o UserKnownHostsFile=
  /dev/null -o StrictHostKeyChecking=no 127.0.0.1
  ```

- Create a new session called pairing:

  ```
  tmux new-session -s pairing
  ```

▥ **Note**   The ssh command to access the VM using the new foo user is quite intense. This is because the default user for the vagrant ssh command is root. You can work around this by modifying the Vagrantfile to include config.ssh.username = "foo" and then running the command vagrant reload to cause the change to take effect. Since you already added the foo user inside the VM, this means you could now use vagrant ssh instead.

Now, in another terminal window, run the following commands, which effectively is us simulating another user on a different computer logging in to the same machine the previous user has logged in to. (If you were trying to apply this to a real-world situation, this would be one in which two users log in to a machine using the same account, and because they're using the same account, they will see the same tmux session.)

- This is the same command as above; we're logging into the VM:

  ```
  ssh -i $(vagrant ssh-config | grep IdentityFile  | awk
  '{print $2}') -l foo -p 2222 -o UserKnownHostsFile=
  /dev/null -o StrictHostKeyChecking=no 127.0.0.1
  ```

- This command isn't necessary; it simply proves the session is available for us to connect to:

  ```
  tmux ls
  ```

- Attach to the relevant tmux session:

  ```
  tmux attach -t pairing
  ```

The downside of this approach is that although two separate users are now able to pair program together using a single tmux session, the users are intrinsically linked; meaning if one user creates a new window, the other user will automatically be focused on that new window (i.e., you can't have one user work independently within his/her own window, although we'll solve this problem in the next section!).

Individual User Control

To solve the problem of two users (logged in under a single shared account) not being able to independently work in a single tmux session is oddly quite simple to achieve. The solution is in how the second user connects to the existing tmux session created by the first user.

When the first user logs into the VM (as the foo user), he/she will create a new tmux session with the following command:

```
tmux new-session -s firstuser
```

When the second user logs in to the VM (again, as the foo user), he/she will create a new session as well, but the difference is that that user will target the other user's session, using the –t flag, like so:

```
tmux new-session -t firstuser -s seconduser
```

Once this is done, both users will be able to see the same windows, but any new windows created occur independently of each user, so one user doesn't automatically get thrown into the new window.

Share Session with Multiple Users

If you would prefer to have users log in to a machine using their own logins but still share a tmux session so they can pair program, the solution is to modify where tmux stores its socket information and assign group access to the new location. We just need to make sure that the individual users are added to the group, so they can access the socket information and thus share the session information.

■ **Note**   You won't be able to work independently inside the tmux session, if using the socket technique (see the next section for a workaround).

The following steps must be carried out before the two users log in to the server. (This is because their user accounts are added to a new group. If you're applying this to a real-world situation, you might not have to create the two user accounts, as they might already exist, and so you'd just need to make sure the user accounts are added to the relevant group.)

- Log into the VM:

  ```
  vagrant ssh
  ```

- Switch to root user (so you can add new users and groups):

  ```
  su
  ```

- Create a new foo user:

  ```
  adduser foo
  ```

- Create a new bar user:

  ```
  adduser bar
  ```

- Create a new baz group:

  ```
  addgroup baz
  ```

- Create a directory to hold our socket data:

  ```
  mkdir /var/qux
  ```

- Apply the baz group to the socket data folder:

  ```
  chgrp baz /var/qux
  ```

- Change the permissions for the socket data folder, which will ensure that any new files added are accessible to the group:

  ```
  chmod g+ws /var/qux
  ```

- Add the foo user to the baz group:

  ```
  usermod -aG baz foo
  ```

- Add the bar user to the baz group:

  ```
  usermod -aG baz bar
  ```

- Switch to the new foo user:

  ```
  su foo
  ```

Now, in another terminal window, run the following commands, which effectively is us simulating another user on a different computer logging in to the same machine the previous user has logged in to, but this time, the user is logging in with his/her own bar account (which was created in the preceding steps):

- Log in to the VM:

  ```
  vagrant ssh
  ```

- Switch to the new bar user:

  ```
  su bar
  ```

Now, at this point, we have two users logged in to the VM under different user accounts. If the foo user were to create a new session using the standard tmux command (i.e., tmux new-session -s mysession), the bar user would still not be able to see that session, because the session was created using the default socket location.

To work around this issue, we have to use the -S (socket-path) flag when creating the session. So, if the foo user executes the following command: tmux -S /var/baz/pairing, he or she will be dropped into a new session, in which the data is stored in a file called pairing.

Now, the bar user can connect to that session, by using the following command: tmux -S /var/baz/pairing attach.

Remotely Accessing a Local VM

Finally, in this section, we'll review some additional features of Vagrant that *can* let us utilize the Vagrant setup and pair program remotely, using Vagrant's sharing functionality (which allows you to share your VM), and will also let us have independent control over tmux windows. The Holy Grail!

For what I'm about to propose to work, the person who is going to share his/her VM has to sign up for a free account with Vagrant (visit https://vagrantcloud.com). Once that person has an account, we'll be able to proceed, by having the person sharing the VM log in to their Vagrant Cloud account via the command line, by executing the vagrant login command.

Once logged in, the same user will share his/her VM by executing the command vagrant share --ssh, which will ask the user to enter a password, to secure the connection. After this is done, Vagrant will display a sample command that you can provide (along with the password) to the user you wish to pair program with. The command will look something like the following:

```
vagrant connect --ssh {dynamically_generated_name}
```

The user who shared his/her VM will have to open a new terminal shell and execute the following commands:

- vagrant ssh: Log in to the VM.

- adduser foo: Create a new shared user.

- su foo: Switch to that user.

- tmux new-session -s foosession: Create a new session.

When the other user you shared the link with has connected to the shared VM, he or she will have to run the following commands:

- su foo: Switch to the new shared user.

- tmux new-session -t groupedsession -s mysession: Create a new session but specify the foosession as their target session.

65

Summary

This has been quite a technically intensive chapter, although it has covered lots of fundamental aspects, to get tmux to bend to your specific requirements. We've used a few different features of Vagrant to help us mimic the situation in which you would ultimately be connecting to a real server (or opened up SSH access on your own machine).

We also demonstrated how Vagrant's built-in VM sharing functionality can help us to work locally on our own machine and to share it with a remote user, while still taking advantage of tmux pair programming with independent control over tmux windows (which is both incredibly powerful and useful).

But if all of that seems like hard work, remember that the third-party tool `http://tmate.io` can take care of all of that hard work for you (with the exception of the independent window access).

CHAPTER 8

■ ■ ■

Workflow Management

Software engineering and web development in particular have changed quite significantly over the past few years. We now have tools at our disposal that would seem almost magical in the past. In this chapter, I am going to demonstrate some of these programs alongside tmux and the Vim text editor, to show you how you can get a more realistic and accurate development environment. I'll also be demonstrating use of the programs Reptyr and tmux-resurrect, so you can see how they fit into your typical workflow.

But before we get into the details of "how," let's consider the "why." What problems are these tools trying to solve? Well, to answer that, we have to know a bit of the history that got us to where we are today. The *traditional* (and massively simplified) web development process would have taken steps that resembled something like the following:

- Open your editor of choice and write code.

- Upload code to your web server.

- Check your application to see if everything worked.

For large organizations, this type of development was fraught with danger and potential downtime to the services they offered their customers, and so this process evolved to include defensive mechanisms, such as writing tests for your code, to ensure fewer bugs made their way into the production environment. The process continued to evolve until we had a set of accepted "best practices," such as, for example, TDD (Test-Driven Development), which was the principle of writing tests first, *before* writing any code, so as to ensure more focused, efficient, and cleaner code.

But all these defensive programming techniques were unable to resolve, arguably, the most fundamental issue that you've likely heard uttered a few times in your career: "but it works on my machine." Effectively, this statement would be uttered by a programmer in the moment of confusion when, after all the tests and checks had passed, and we were "all systems go," we would proceed to upload the application to the server and watch as certain aspects of the software failed to work as intended.

The reason for this is that we weren't developing our applications in an environment that accurately represented the live server environment. How can you ever know for sure whether your application will work, if you're developing it on a Mac- or Windows-based operating system, and yet its destination is a Linux server whose architecture is sufficiently different to cause even simple errors, such as "case sensitivity."

Because of this issue, tools such as Vagrant (`http://vagrantup.com`) stepped in to try and resolve the problem, by providing software engineers a common ground to work from. With a tool such as Vagrant, you can replicate your live server environment, by creating a new virtual machine that runs the same operating system and software packages, as well as utilizing the same provisioning scripts as would your live server. At this point, I would recommend visiting the web site and downloading/installing the version of Vagrant that is most relevant to your operating system.

Example Repository

To make things easier, and to save on having to type it all out yourself, you can download a fully working development environment that includes all the topics, techniques, and software that I'm about to describe to you. You should be able to run the following Git command to download the project:

```
git clone https://github.com/Integralist/Linux-and-Docker-Development-
Environment.git
```

Once inside the cloned directory, you should notice a file called `Vagrantfile`. This file is what Vagrant uses to configure the development environment. As long as you have Vagrant installed, you can run the `vagrant up` command from your terminal, to create the environment. (When you run the command, make sure you are inside the directory that contains the `Vagrantfile`.) This will cause VirtualBox to trigger a new instance of the development environment, which, in this case, is a Ubuntu-based Linux server, to be started.

▓ **Note** This is a mini-book about tmux, so I won't be explaining how the code in the `Vagrantfile` or the provisioning script works (although both are heavily commented, so you should be able to get by).

What we should end up with is an Ubuntu instance that has Vim, tmux, and Git installed, along with the Reptyr program. We should also have Docker (`www.docker.com`) installed and a container created that runs our application (in this example, it's a "Hello World" Ruby application). Docker is a solution for building modular and distributed applications.

Reptyr

The Reptyr program allows you to attach to your tmux session processes that are already running (or, in fact, any terminal multiplexer, such as screen). This can be really useful in situations in which you have some long-running process that is already running by the time you come to log on to the server. Instead of having to stop and start the process (and subsequently losing any important information it may have gathered), you can open tmux and reattach the process so it's now running inside tmux.

The way it works is complicated. If you're really interested in the implementation details, I recommend that you read the documentation on the GitHub repository at `https://github.com/nelhage/reptyr`.

To see an example of how this works, we must log in to the VM (virtual machine) that Vagrant has brought up for us. To do this, you'll run the command `vagrant ssh`, and from that point, you'll be able to complete the remaining steps, which are as follows (i.e., execute each step as a separate command):

- `top`

- `<C-z>`

- `bg`

- `disown top`

- `tmux`

- `reptyr $(pgrep top)`

If you have followed the preceding steps, you should have a tmux session open, and the `top` program (which was originally started *before* you created the tmux session) has been successfully moved inside tmux.

Let's now go through each of the preceding steps one by one, to clarify what we've done. First, we started a new instance of the `top` program, which displays information about running processes on our VM. Next, we suspended the `top` program by running the command `<C-z>`. (This temporarily suspends the process from running but keeps it alive, so we can resume it later.)

We then ran the `bg` command to convert the last process (`top`, in this case) into a background process. The reason we do that is so the next step can be taken, which is to run the `disown top` command (the `disown` command disassociates the specified process with its parent process). The reason for disowning the process is to allow us to re-associate it with the tmux process.

Next, we start a new tmux session, and within tmux, we run the command `reptyr $(pgrep top)`, which passes the result of the `pgrep top` command (the result being the process id for the `top` program) into the Reptyr program, causing the `top` program to be placed into our tmux session.

tmux-resurrect

The tmux-resurrect plug-in gives you the ability to restore the state of tmux, even after a system restart. It does this by recording all your data at the point of executing a specific tmux key binding and restoring the data when running a specific tmux key binding.

Although this plug-in can be extremely useful, you might be wondering why I don't install it by default as part of my "Linux and Docker Development Environment" GitHub repository? The reason for this decision is that the plug-in has limited use in a disposable workflow environment (i.e., one with no persistent storage).

What I mean by that is, if I was using tmux (and this plug-in) directly on the host machine (i.e., on my Mac OS), it would be useful, because when I shut down my Mac at the end of a workday and then start it up again in the morning, I have a persistent storage drive, which means I'll be able to restore my tmux sessions.

But when you're working from a virtual environment, you don't have persistent storage in the same way, and so when you shut down a VM and restart it, the entire operating system is rebuilt from scratch. But this isn't to say this isn't a useful plug-in to have installed on your main host machine (as I don't just use tmux from within a VM; I use it all the time on my Mac OS).

Installation

To install the plug-in, you'll have to first download the repository, using the following command (we download the code into `~/tmux/plugins/resurrect`):

```
git clone https://github.com/tmux-plugins/tmux-resurrect
~/tmux/plugins/resurrect
```

Once we have the plug-in downloaded, we can tell tmux to load it, by adding the following command into the `.tmux.conf` file:

```
run-shell ~/tmux/plugins/resurrect/resurrect.tmux
```

If tmux is already running, I suggest you source the `.tmux.conf` file, by executing the `source-file ~/.tmux.conf` command.

▩ **Note**   There are many additional settings that you can enable, such as restoring Vim sessions (e.g., `set -g @resurrect-strategy-vim 'session'`). I recommend reading the plug-in documentation for the full details.

Sample Usage

Using the plug-in is very easy. Once you have tmux open and in a state that you want to record, execute the key binding `<P><C-s>`, to store the current layout and contents.

Once you restart the machine (you can mimic this by executing the tmux command `<P>:kill-server`) and open tmux afresh, you'll notice that the state is lost. To resume the previous state, simply execute the key binding `<P><C-r>`, and after a brief moment, you should see your earlier layout.

Summary

We've finally arrived to the end of the last chapter. I've hoped you've enjoyed yourself. Everything that you've learned from this book is merely the beginning.

The true joy of using tools such as tmux is that there is so much more to learn and to utilize. As you become more and more confident with the tooling, you'll discover new ways to take advantage of them.

I would enjoy very much hearing your feedback, so feel free to open discussions and comments at https://github.com/Integralist/ProVim. But for now, let's take a moment to look back on what we have seen in this final chapter.

- At the start of the chapter, I briefly discussed the evolution of a traditional development process and how certain practices were put in place to ensure consistency between development and production environments. (This is where such tools as VirtualBox and Vagrant were introduced.)

- We moved on to downloading an example repository that with a single command (i.e., vagrant up) would be able to re-create a complete Linux environment, with development tools installed and ready to use, thereby demonstrating the power of having a virtual workspace that is completely deposable and configurable to match a live production environment.

- From there, we took a look at the Reptyr program and how it is useful for attaching existing processes to another process (in this case, tmux), so that we don't have to worry about losing any state we may have accumulated before running tmux.

- We also looked at the tmux-resurrect plug-in, which demonstrates how tmux's layout and content (even down to individual panes and Vim context) can be persisted through a system restart. Powerful tooling, indeed.

Index

Get the eBook for only $10!

Now you can take the weightless companion with you anywhere, anytime. Your purchase of this book entitles you to 3 electronic versions for only $10.

This Apress title will prove so indispensible that you'll want to carry it with you everywhere, which is why we are offering the eBook in 3 formats for only $10 if you have already purchased the print book.

Convenient and fully searchable, the PDF version enables you to easily find and copy code—or perform examples by quickly toggling between instructions and applications. The MOBI format is ideal for your Kindle, while the ePUB can be utilized on a variety of mobile devices.

Go to www.apress.com/promo/tendollars to purchase your companion eBook.